Mila.. w.th
Lakes Como
& Maggiore

Lara Dunston & Terry Carter

Credits

Footprint credits
Editor: Jo Williams
Production and layout: Emma Bryers
Maps: Kevin Feeney
Cover: Pepi Bluck

Publisher: Patrick Dawson
Managing Editor: Felicity Laughton
Advertising: Elizabeth Taylor
Sales and marketing: Kirsty Holmes

Photography credits
Front cover: Adriano Castelli/
Shutterstock.com
Back cover: Alexander Chaikin/
Shutterstock.com

Printed in Great Britain by CPI Antony Rowe,
Chippenham, Wiltshire

MIX
Paper from
responsible sources
FSC® C013604
www.fsc.org

Publishing information
Footprint *Focus Milan with Lakes Como*
& Maggiore
1st edition
© Footprint Handbooks Ltd
March 2013

ISBN: 978 1 908206 93 0
CIP DATA: A catalogue record for this book
is available from the British Library

® Footprint Handbooks and the Footprint
mark are a registered trademark of
Footprint Handbooks Ltd

Published by Footprint
6 Riverside Court
Lower Bristol Road
Bath BA2 3DZ, UK
T +44 (0)1225 469141
F +44 (0)1225 469461
footprinttravelguides.com

Distributed in the USA by Globe Pequot
Press, Guilford, Connecticut

The content of Footprint *Focus Milan with
Lakes Como & Maggiore* has been taken
directly from Footprint's *Italian Lakes* guide,
which was researched and written by
Lara Dunston and Terry Carter.

Contents

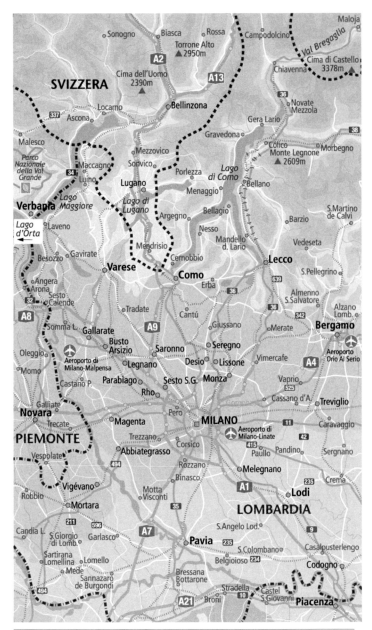

Milan can appear to be a dispassionate capital of cool, where the blinkered worlds of fashion, design and finance take precedence over the Italian notion of living *la dolce vita*. However, while it may be the city that drives the Italian economy, it also takes time out to appreciate the sweet life. Once work is over, the Milanese know how and where to relax; they did, after all, invent the *aperitivo* ritual – they just plan it like a military operation. The world-famous La Scala theatre, splendid museums and galleries, and fine-dining restaurants featuring the wonderful wines and produce of northern Italy are all a focus of Milanese life – as they should be for your stay too!

But when the weekend and holidays arrive, the Milanese and residents of other towns and cities of the region know that their reward is right on their doorsteps: the treasures that are the Italian Lakes. With their grand hotels, luxuriant villa gardens, boating, biking and hiking, brilliant restaurants and laid-back cafés and bars, the lakes are the reward for the hard-working northern Italians. Near every lake there is a wonderful town or village to explore, such as Como with its elegant old hotels, imposing marble Duomo, labyrinthine *centro storico* and lovely views of the lake, and Bellagio, a breathtakingly beautiful village with lush parks and elegant gardens, charming stores on skinny lanes and romantic waterfront restaurants. Hard work, after all, should have its pay-offs.

Best time to visit Milan and Lakes Como and Maggiore

Spring and autumn are lovely but, despite the crowds and sticky heat, summer is best of all. June marks the start of the summer season with plenty of events to celebrate it. **Festa del Naviglio** (see page 14) sees Milan's Navigli come alive with concerts and markets, while **Milano d'Estate** (see page 14) offers concerts in Parco Sempione and Castello Sforzesco. On the lakes, the **Festa di San Giovanni** (see page 14) sees spectacular fireworks on Isola Comacina. Long lines of terrific-looking men outside designers' ateliers signal the start of men's fashion week. By July, summer is in full swing and so is Milan's nightlife though shopping excursions can be thwarted by the heat – stay hydrated. The lakes are fantastic with festivals and events wherever you float your boat. Book accommodation well ahead. Milan is dead in August, when locals go on holidays. Remember that the month of August is also quite hot and humid in Milan so the vibe is infinitely better on the lakes, but it's very crowded with tourists, so book well ahead. In September, Monza becomes the centre of the Formula One world with the Grand Prix and the women's spring/summer fashion week fills restaurants, bars and hotel rooms. Foodies love winter when restaurants serve hearty, warming dishes. Two of Milan's biggest events take place in December: **Festa di Sant'Ambrogio** (Milan's patron saint) (see page 15) and the start of opera season at **La Scala** – get tickets in advance and pack glamorous. While the lakes can be pretty in winter, they're also deserted. Many hotels and restaurants close up completely for the season and places such as Bellagio are like ghost towns.

Getting to Milan and Lakes Como and Maggiore

Air
From UK and Ireland Access to the lakes is gained by overland travel after arriving in the following cities: Milan (closest to Maggiore and Como), Bergamo (Como), Brescia (Como) and Lugano in Switzerland (Maggiore, Como).

From North America **Alitalia**, **American Airlines**, **British Airways** and **Delta** are some of the airlines offering direct flights from the States to **Milan Malpensa Airport**. Many Canadian travellers will have to either change in the US, or fly to another European city for a connection. **Alitalia** fly directly from Toronto to Rome. A popular route from North America to Milan is via Dubai, travelling with **Emirates**.

From rest of Europe Direct flights to the airports serving northern Italy depart from all major European cities. There are direct passenger trains to Milano Centrale from many points of departure including Munich, Paris and Amsterdam. A **Motorail** ① *www.raileurope. co.uk/frenchmotorail*, service carries passengers and their vehicles from Düsseldorf to Verona. The Motorail service – a car-carrying train – has advantages over combining a flight with car hire. You can carry as much luggage as you want and bring back as much as you like. An overnight long distance motorail journey can be time effective compared with a flight and the sleeper can even save on a hotel bill or two. There aren't yet any direct motorail trains to Italy from France, but a service departs from Calais to Nice, leaving about a four hour drive along the Southern French coast and up to the Italian lakes.

Airport information **Milan Malpensa Airport** ① *www.milanomalpensa1.eu*, just 15 km from Lake Maggiore, is well placed for access to the western lakes. There's a bus to central

Best of Milan and Lakes Como and Maggiore

Duomo You'll find yourself circling this colossal cathedral time and again to gawk at its 3400 intricately carved statues, but don't miss its lofty rooftop, where the views of Milan are spectacular. Page 20.

Teatro alla Scala Milan's sumptuous opera theatre, with its gilded balconies and plush private boxes, is one of the world's most magnificent. Page 26.

Quadrilatero d'Oro Fashionistas and shopaholics understandably make a beeline for Milan's famous fashion quarter, but a visit is vital even for those uninterested in shopping. The cobblestone streets are charming and the window displays jaw-dropping. Page 37.

Lombardy's gastronomic restaurants Dining is one of the real delights of the area; restaurant highlights include chef Pietro Leemann's vegetarian Joia in Milan and Antonino Cannavacciuolo's exotic Villa Crespi on Lake Orta. Pages 48 and 87.

Lake Como Cruising on or around romantic Lake Como, by boat, bike or car, is addictive, while Como is one of Northern Italy's most sophisticated towns. Page 60.

Lake Orta Its shores lined with graceful villas and verdant gardens, this tiny cobalt blue lake must be Italy's most alluring. Page 85.

Milan every 20 minutes (journey time 50 minutes, €10) and the Malpensa Express train every 30 minutes (40 minutes to Cadorna station, €11). Change midway at Saronno for lines heading north to Como and Maggiore. **Linate Airport** ① *T02-748 5220, www.milanolinate.eu*, 15 km east of Milan, is connected to San Babila station by city bus 73 every 10 minutes (30 minutes, €1). **Orio al Serio Airport** ① *www.sacbo.it*, 8 km southeast of Bergamo, is a gateway to Como.

Rail
You can travel with **Eurostar** ① *www.eurostar.com*, from London to Paris before joining an overnight sleeper from Paris Bercy to Verona Porta Nuova. Book tickets at **www.raileurope.com**. When making transfers to the lakes, the major towns are: Como/Varenna/Lecco for Lake Como; Arona/Stresa/Verbania for Lake Maggiore.

Road
It's a 1200 km journey from London to the most westerly lake, Orta, but you'll be treated to some amazing scenery. If it's high-octane you're after, take the Stelvio Pass, 100 km north of Garda: with 48 hairpin turns, Jeremy Clarkson rates it as the best drive in the world. EU nationals taking their own car need an International Insurance Certificate (also known as a Green Card). Those holding a non-EU licence also need to take an International Driving Permit. **Autostrade** ① *T055-420 3200, www.autostrade.it*, provides information on Italian motorways and **Automobile Club Italiana** ① *T06-49981, www.aci.it*, gives general driving information.

Bus/coach Eurolines ① *T08717-818178, www.nationalexpress.co.uk*, operate three services per week from London Victoria to Milan with a travel time of around 28 hours. Prices start at £124 return. Coaches arrive and depart in Milan at the bus station Milano Lampugnano.

Transport in Milan and Lakes Como and Maggiore

There are several options for getting around Milan and the Lakes – if you want to do plenty of sightseeing, visiting many of the towns covered in the book, by car is the best way to do it. If you are planning on driving, a good map to take is the AA Road Map *Italy: Italian Lakes & Milan*. If you just want to go from say, Milan to Lake Como and hang out, it's easy to just catch the train and do sightseeing by ferry. If you're planning on doing some hiking or off-road mountain biking, it's best to get trail maps from the actual destination, either from the tourist office or a climbing/biking shop.

Rail
Italy has an extensive rail network, and it's the best way to get around the country on a city-based trip. It's often quicker than a domestic flight, when you include check-in times and waiting for baggage. Milan to Rome, for instance, takes just over four hours. There is good rail coverage in the north of Italy and you can cover many of the places listed in this book by train.

It's worth knowing that there are several different train services running in Italy: air-conditioned and splendid Eurostar Italia, direct and convenient InterCity, and the slightly less regular Regional trains. All can be booked at www.trenitalia.com, where the type of train is indicated with the initials ES, IC or REG. 'Amica' fares are cheaper advance tickets (if you can find one), flexi fare costs more but is – you guessed it – flexible, and standard fare is just that.

In general, it's cheaper and more convenient to book online or at ticket machines for the journeys you need to take than it is to buy a pass. When using a service such as Eurostar Italia or InterCity, booking is advised and a surcharge in addition to a pass will often be required; passes therefore lose their thrift factor for tourists. On many Italian trains it's possible to travel 'ticketless', meaning you get on the train and quote your booking reference when the conductor comes round.

Booking and buying tickets at the counter or via machines in train stations is convenient if you can't access the internet. Remember, you must validate train tickets at the yellow stamping machines before boarding.

Road
EU nationals taking their own car need to have an International Insurance Certificate (also known as a Carte Verde). Those holding a non-EU licence also need to take an International Driving Permit with them. Unleaded petrol is *benzina*, diesel is *gasolio*.

Italy has strict laws on drink driving – steer clear of alcohol to be safe. The use of mobile telephones while driving is illegal. Other nuances of Italian road law include children under 1.5 m being required to be in the back of the car and a reflective jacket must be worn if your car breaks down on the carriageway in poor visibility. Make sure you've got one. Since July 2007 on-the-spot fines for minor traffic offences have been in operation – typically €150-250. Always get a receipt if you incur one.

Speed limits are 130 kph (motorway), 110 kph (dual carriageway) and 50 kph (town). Limits are 20 kph lower on motorways and dual carriageways when the road is wet.

Autostrade (motorways) are toll roads, so keep cash in the car as a backup even though you can use credit cards on the blue 'viacard' gates. **Autostrade** ① *T840 04 21 21, www. autostrade.it*, provides information on motorways in Italy and **Automobile Club d'Italia** ① *T803 116, www.aci.it*, provides general driving information. ACI offers roadside assistance with English-speaking operators on T116.

Be aware that there are restrictions on driving in historic city centres, indicated by signs with black letters ZTL (*zona a traffico limitato*) on a yellow background. If you pass these signs, your registration number may be caught and a fine winging its way to you. If your hotel is in the centre of town, you may be entitled to an official pass – contact your hotel or car hire company. However, this pass is not universal and only allows access to the hotel.

Car hire Car hire is available at all of Italy's international airports and many domestic airports. You will probably wish to book the car hire before you arrive in the country, and it's best to do so for popular destinations and at busy times of year. Check in advance the opening times of the car hire office.

Car hire comparison websites and agents are a good place to start a search for the best deals. Try www.easycar.com or www.carrentals.co.uk.

Check what each hire company requires from you. Some companies will ask for an International Driving Licence, alongside your normal driving licence, if the language of your driving licence is different to the country you're renting the car in. Others are content with an EU licence. You'll need to produce a credit card for virtually all companies. If you book ahead, make sure that the named credit card holder is the same as the person renting and driving the car to avoid any problems. Most companies have a lower age limit of 21 years and require that you've held your licence for at least a year. Many have a young driver surcharge for those under 25. Confirm insurance and any damage waiver charges and keep all your documents with you when you drive. Always take a printed copy of the contract with you, regardless of whether you have a booking number and a 'confirmed' booking.

Bicycle While Milan itself is not the easiest city to ride a bike in, thankfully the rest of the areas covered by this book are. While the roads are narrow, Italians love their bike-riding and are well used to passing cyclists. Bikes can be hired everywhere on the lakes and mountain bikes are available at the popular mountain-biking destinations.

Bus/coach While you can use buses to get around, trains (often with a convenient link to the city centres by bus) are more popular.

Where to stay in Milan and Lakes Como and Maggiore

The region offers a wide variety of accommodation, from stylish designer digs in Milan catering for the fashionistas, to romantic grand hotels on the lakes. While accommodation for budget travellers is patchy, mid-range and luxury travellers will have no problem finding accommodation that suits them in the destinations covered in this book.

Where to sleep

The best way to decide what kind of hotel to stay in is to align it with the theme of your visit. If you're in Milan for shopping in the Quadrilatero D'Oro (the shopping district), stick close to this exclusive quarter and stay in a place where your designer shopping bags will be lifted from your weary arms and magically appear in your room before you can order a glass of champagne. If you're design-focused, deconstruct one of the glossy, minimalist hotels. If you're after romance, nothing beats a grand old hotel or whimsical villa on a lake's shore or a charismatic *albergo* in the centre of a historic town such as Como. If it's a family holiday, then you might want to consider renting an apartment or camping in one of the lakeside holiday parks.

Deciding on the location of a hotel is easy. In Milan, the centre or the shopping district is perfect to get a feel for the city sights and shopping, the Brera area is great if you're an art and antiques lover, and the Navigli is ideal if you want a more down-to-earth feel and a great choice of local restaurants and bars – especially in summer. On the lakes, anything with a view is better than none, and the grander the hotel the better. And while there are certainly some swish hotels lining the lakes' shores, grand doesn't have to mean luxe. For those travelling with children or on a budget there are some wonderful old piles that fall into the two- or three-star category that ooze charm. There are also great value apartments in the centres of cities and towns for those self-catering, and cosy B&Bs and tranquil *agriturismo* options smattered throughout the region.

What to expect

On paper, Italy has a star classification system akin to other European countries, but the reality on the ground doesn't quite reflect the ratings. Amenities that have been listed often don't exist or don't work and sometimes you'll find staff more interested in looking good than looking after their guests. The hotels are graded from one- to five-star deluxe, but a well-run, well-positioned three-star can often offer a better experience than a five-star filled with self-absorbed staff or a position on the outskirts of the town centre.

In one- and two-star hotels (sometimes called *pensioni*) you often have to share bathrooms, but some of these properties can be full of atmosphere, with genial hosts. The three-star options almost always have an en suite bathroom and air conditioning – strongly recommended for the sticky summers. Many four-star options in Milan generally cater for business travellers and are quite anodyne, but there are a few boutique properties in this range that have unique decor, if not conscientious staff. The five-star hotels in Milan are generally excellent, with attentive service, flat-screen TVs and champagne waiting to be popped in a well-stocked minibar, while many of the five-stars on the lakes offer faded charm, old-school glamour, and glorious views. If a place is described as an *albergo,* these days it simply means a hotel and it can have any star rating. Similarly with a *locanda,* which traditionally referred to an inn or a restaurant with rooms. A bed and breakfast can simply be a room in someone's residence (for better or worse) or can mean a charming stay in a lovely cottage or cabin where only breakfast is served.

Price codes

Where to stay

€€€€ over €300   €€€ €200-300

€€ €100-200   € under €100

Price codes refer to the cost of a double room in high season.

Restaurants

€€€ over €40   €€ €20-40   € under €20

Price codes refer to the cost of a two-course meal with a drink, including service and cover charge.

While *agriturismi* – that is, rural accommodation or rooms on a working farm or vineyard – are hugely popular in regions such as Tuscany and Umbria, the trend has been slower to take off in the lakes area where the grand hotel experience dominates. If you're determined to seek out such experiences in this part of Italy, do your research carefully as many properties are based on a great idea but the experiences are poorly executed; see www.loveitaly.co.uk and www.agriturist.it for some of the best examples.

If you are intending to spend more than a week in one place and you're not planning on bugging the concierge every 15 minutes for directions or restaurant bookings, seriously consider renting an apartment for your stay. Not only will you save money if you're looking at anything from mid-range or above, but shopping for groceries at the local markets and living like a local in a city that you want to get to know better can be just as enjoyable and rewarding as seeing a major attraction you've always dreamt of visiting.

What you get for your euros

While some of the hotels mentioned in this book have great restaurants (and a couple are worth staying at for the cuisine alone), you'll find that breakfasts in all but the five-star hotels are generally a fairly simple affair of good coffee and tiny pastries – Italians are not big on hot breakfasts and it's unusual to find elaborate buffets anywhere but in the very best luxury hotels.

Whether or not a hotel has parking is worth considering if your trip involves driving around the lakes. Don't even think about hiring a car for Milan, as parking is a challenge. If you're staying in Milan before heading off to the lakes, as many travellers do, then pick the car up on your way out and drop it off on your way back. Outside of Milan, hotels that have parking (especially if they are located in the centre of the city or town) are advantageous, as many towns don't have street parking in the historic centre. Always check parking arrangements and pricing with the hotel when you book your accommodation, as the hotel garages can often be tricky to locate and some close early and on Sundays.

Something else to consider if you need to work or simply stay in touch with family and friends while you travel is the availability of the internet in hotels. Regardless of whether it's advertised or not, in-room Wi-Fi can be expected to be delivered about as often as it snows in Milan (hint: not often); broadband is the better option if available. Unfortunately, the hotels that deliver the most reliable internet are generally the bland four- and five-star business hotels, for obvious reasons. Most other hotels rely on outside providers to deploy and run the internet services in the hotel and the lack of a connection is often treated with a shrug that would do the French proud. For those who need to do business while travelling, your best bets are the upmarket chains that will have a functioning business centre and reasonably good internet access. Elsewhere access is sporadic at the best of times, and expensive.

Food and drink in Milan and Lakes Como and Maggiore

Dining and imbibing in the Italian Lakes is an absolute joy, with interesting local dishes dotted throughout the region, and wonderfully distinctive wines. Just like the rest of Italy, you don't have to haunt haute cuisine restaurants to have a satisfying meal – often the simplest dish at the most basic *enoteca* (wine bar) can be something special. The wines of northern Italy stand tall in any company with the big standout red, Barolo, appearing on most wine lists in the region.

Local specialities
Lombardy – and also Piedmont, which the lakes area falls within – have an interesting gastronomic pedigree, with mountains, valleys and sweeping plains offering diverse terrain for cultivation, providing a wide range of recipes. Dishes tend to be heavier in the north, with more use of butter and cream rather than just olive oil. One of the dishes that defines the region is the Milanese dish *ossobuco* (slow-braised veal shanks) served with *risotto alla milanese* (rice with saffron threads). While breaded veal cutlets (*cotoletta alla milanese*) might appear to be influenced by the Austrians, with its apparent connection to *wiener schnitzel*, but was in fact created much earlier.

Given that Milan is the largest centre, it's not surprising that regional specialities from all over the north (not just Milan and the lakes) appear widely on menus. You'll typically see dishes from Genoa, which gives us *pesto alla genovese* (classic basil pesto), Modena, which exports its wonderful *aceto balsamico* (balsamic vinegar), Parma, which kindly lets the rest of us try its brilliant hams and Parmigiano-Reggiano cheese, and arguably most famous of all, Bologna, which gives us its *ragù alla bolognese* (Bolognese sauce). Specialities also include *bresaola di Valtellina* (air-cured, thinly sliced beef from the Valtellina area near Switzerland) and *polenta*, a cornmeal peasant staple that has found favour again in the best restaurants of the world.

Local wines
Just as in France, the region from which wine comes provides one of the most important characteristics of the tipple, and the Italians have a wine categorization system comparable to that of France. In the Lombardy region, much of the production goes to making table wines; however, the sparkling wines of Franciacorta are arguably the best in Italy, along with the Nebbiolo grape's reds, grown on the steep slopes of the Valtellina region.

The Piedmont region is home to Italy's superstar wine, Barolo, and the wineries of the region are more 'boutique' affairs. Barolo is a big red made from the local Nebbiolo grapes and it's one that is best left to age for a few years, and it can drink well for 20 years and beyond. Barbaresco is the less famous, and more affordable, brother of Barolo and drinks well at an earlier age.

Types of eateries
The demarcation of eateries in Italy is quite complex, but as you'll see from the recommendations in this book, an *enoteca* (wine bar) can offer just as satisfying a meal as a restaurant. A *ristorante* is an establishment with linen tablecloths, formal waiters,

and no prices on the menus for the women, and hefty prices on the menu for the gentlemen. A *trattoria* is more casual than a *ristorante* and usually has a seasonal menu with local specialities and often pan-Italian favourites. Both are generally open for lunch (approximately 1200-1500) and dinner (1900-2200), closing in between. An *osteria* is a small eatery with a short, focused menu and wine list, generally featuring local specialities and is usually only open in the evening. An *enoteca* is a wine bar that will have a few dishes or just great local cheeses and cold meats served on platters – an excellent substitute for dinner if you're still struggling after a big lunch. A café serves coffee, drinks and sandwiches, as does the more pared-back, unpretentious bar, and these usually stay open all day and night, opening early and closing late. A pizzeria, of course, sells pizza, but a guide to the good ones will be the words *forno a legna* (wood-fired oven) somewhere near its name.

Shopping and markets

Stalls laden with freshly picked fruit and vegetables, specialist vans selling cheeses and meats, cases of table wines sold off the back of a truck … market shopping in the Italian Lakes is truly first class. With fruit and vegetables, if it's in season it's in stock, if it's not then you're out of luck. Salamies, most cheeses, and breads are never out of season. The same goes for wonderful wines and preserves – all perfect for a picnic. When shopping for food, keep in mind that some items may not be allowed through customs when you return home, so enjoy it while you're here!

Vegetarian options

Vegetarians are in luck anywhere in Italy, with plenty of wonderful pasta dishes and pizzas on menus that do not contain meat, as well as brilliant grilled vegetables. Salads, polenta, beans and risottos are excellent without *carne* (meat) as well.

From food and wine, fashion and furniture to the Formula One, Milan and the lakes offer a diverse array of festivals and events sprinkled liberally throughout the year. Even if you're not into the reason for the celebration, you won't be able to resist joining in. You'll find the streets alive with people – even the hard-working northern Italians love an excuse to have a break and relax. Keep in mind though that accommodation around events such as the fashion weeks is reserved months in advance and restaurants can be fully booked.

Festivals in Milan and Lakes Como and Maggiore

January
Corteo dei Re Magi (**6th**) Epiphany is a public holiday and is celebrated with the 'Wise Men Processional', a traditional Nativity procession, moving from Milan's Duomo to Sant'Eustagio. The children are happy because they get more festive presents – if they're good.

February
Carnevale Ambrosiano Milan's Carnevale – the world's longest carnival – ends with a parade to piazza del Duomo. It's a great one for the kids, who roam the streets in fancy dress causing old-fashioned mischief (www.comune.milano.it).

Milano Moda Donna Autunno/Inverno Held in late Feb, this is the fashion show of the year, with the best designers draping their autumn/winter collections over the skeletal frames of girls just out of high school. Aperitivo bars and restaurants are buzzing and celebrity spotting becomes an addictive activity.

March
Milano Internazionale Antiquariato This renowned international antique show, held over four days at the Fiera di Milano, is one of the highlights of the arts and antiquities calendar worldwide. Held late Mar–early Apr, biennially on even-numbered years.

April
Liberation Day (**25th**) Celebrated all over Italy, it marks the liberation of Italy by allied troops in the Second World War.

Salone Internazionale del Mobile Europe's massive furniture fair has a day for the public (Sun) where you can salivate over the latest home furnishings and design. Milan has a tangible buzz during the fair.

June
Festa del Naviglio Milan's Navigli area comes to life for summer with 10 days of concerts and performances, cooking, arts and the renowned antique market (also held on the last Sun of every month).

Festival Mix The Festival Mix Milano (www.festivalmixmilano.com) is an engaging week-long celebration of gay and lesbian film and queer culture – brush up on your Italian though, as most of the films don't have English subtitles.

Milano d'Estate Concerts in Parco Sempione and Castello Sforzesco over the summer months go some way in making up for Milan's muggy heat for those unable to escape to the beach.

Festa di San Giovanni (**24th**) Fireworks are the highlight of a day of celebrations on Isola Comacina for St John.

July
Notturni in Villa This series of free concerts in Milan's beautiful city villas feature an eclectic mix of genres, but mainly focuses on jazz and classical music.

Festival Latino Americando 2 months (Jul-Aug) of celebrating Latin American culture in Milan, with plenty of food, dancing and music at various venues around the city (www.latinoamericando.it).

August
Ferragosto (**15th**) The Feast of the Assumption is celebrated all over the country with gusto – by doing as little as possible and eating as much as possible. For some it's the start of the summer holiday, for others it's the halfway mark.

September
Festival Milano A festival of contemporary music, dance and theatre, with events ongoing through to Oct.

Italian Formula One Grand Prix This very popular round of the Formula One circus is beloved by the F1 drivers who enjoy the challenge of the high-speed Monza track and the fanatical Italian Ferrari fans who make this an annual pilgrimage, complete with giant red flags (www.monzanet.it).

October
Milano International Film
Festival Featuring full-length features and documentaries, short films and retrospectives (www.milanofilmfestival.it).
Milano Marathon Starting and ending at the imposing Castello Sforzesco, the flat course makes for fast times on the cobbled streets (www.milanocitymarathon.gazzetta.it).

November
Tutti Santi (1st) All Saints' Day is a public holiday with numerous religious celebrations. Italians traditionally enjoy a harvest feast, give presents to their children, and attend a special mass.

December
Festa di Sant'Ambrogio (7th)
Throughout the region this is the public holiday to celebrate Milan's patron saint, St Ambrose. Piazza Sant'Ambrogio and the surrounding streets are the focus of attention, with stalls selling everything from chestnuts to cured meats.
La Scala Season Opening (7th) Coinciding with the Feast of Sant'Ambrogio is the opening of Milan's famous opera season. Perhaps the biggest night on the Milanese social calendar, tickets to the opening opera are hard to come by.

Essentials A-Z

Customs and immigration
UK and EU citizens do not need a visa, but will need a valid passport to enter Italy. A standard tourist visa for those outside of the EU is valid for up to 90 days.

Disabled travellers
Italy is a bit behind when it comes to catering for disabled travellers, where access is sometimes very difficult or ill thought out. Contact an association or agency before departure for more details such as **Accessible Italy**, www.accessibleitaly.com, or **Society for Accessible Travel and Hospitality**, www.sath.org. Locally, **Milano Per Tutti**, www.milanopertutti.it, has an extensive database (available in English or Italian) of sights in the city and important information such as door widths. A non-profit organization, **A.I.A.S. di Milano ONLUS** (via Mantegazza Paolo 10, T02-330 2021, www.aiasmilano.it), runs the website.

Electricity
Italy functions on a 220V mains supply and the standard European 2-pin plug.

Emergency numbers
Police T112 (with English-speaking operators), T113 (carabinieri); **Ambulance** T118; **Fire** T115; **Roadside assistance** T116.

Etiquette
Bella figura – projecting a good image – is important to Italians. Smart casual dress at the very least is expected, even in summer when other countries dress down. Take note of public notices about conduct: sitting on steps or eating and drinking in certain historic areas is not allowed. Covering arms and legs is necessary for admission into some churches – in some cases shorts are not permitted. Punctuality is apparently not mandatory in Italy, so be prepared to wait on occasion – even at government-run sights where opening times are often treated as a suggestion.

Families
Whether for a traditional beach break or an afternoon in a gelateria, families are well accommodated in Italy. The family is highly regarded in Italy and bambini are indulged, and there's plenty to do for children besides endless museum visits. Do note that sometimes lone parents or adults accompanying children of a different surname may need evidence before taking children in and out of the country. Contact your Italian embassy for current details (Italian embassy in London, T020-7312 2200).

Health
Comprehensive travel and medical insurance is strongly recommended for all travel. EU citizens should apply for a free European Health Insurance Card (ehic.org.uk) which replaced the E111 form and offers reduced-cost medical treatment. Late-night pharmacies are identified by a large green cross outside. T1100 for addresses of three nearest open pharmacies. The accident and emergency department of a hospital is the pronto soccorso. Local hospital details are in the Directory sections for each destination.

Insurance
Comprehensive travel and medical insurance is strongly recommended for all travel – the EHIC is not a replacement for insurance. You should check any exclusions, and that your policy covers you for all the activities you want to undertake. Keep details of your insurance documents separately; emailing yourself with the details is a good way to keep the information safe and accessible. Ensure you have full insurance if hiring a car, and you might need an international insurance

certificate if taking your own car (contact your current insurers).

Money

The Italian currency is the euro. There are ATMs throughout Italy that accept major credit and debit cards. To change cash or traveller's cheques, look for a cambio. Most restaurants, shops, museums and art galleries take major credit cards. Paying directly with debit cards such as Cirrus is less easy in some places, so withdrawing from an ATM and paying cash is the better option. Keep plenty of cash for toll roads if you're driving. ATMs are everywhere in the region.

Cost of living

Allow an absolute minimum of €100 per day per person if eating and sleeping on a budget, sharing accommodation and self-catering, and a minimum of €250 per person per day for a taste of Milan and the lakes' luxe life. While accommodation is rarely a bargain here, skipping dinner at the expensive restaurants, and opting for fixed price lunch menus, snacking standing at a bar like the locals, and doing some self-catering from the mouth-watering delicatessens, can keep budget travellers happy. Unless you're taking sporting lessons or hiring a yacht, water-based activities are quite reasonably priced on the lakes.

Police

While it appears that there are several different types of police in Italy (and several dozen uniforms for each!), there are 2 types of police forces that you will see most often: the **polizia** (T113) and the **carabinieri** (T112). The polizia are the 'normal' police under the control of the Interior Ministry, while the carabinieri are a defacto military force. However both will respond if you need help.

Post

Italian post has a not entirely undeserved reputation for being unreliable, particularly for handling postcards. Overseas post will require *posta prioritaria* (priority mail) and a postcard stamp will start at €0.85. You can buy *francobolli* (stamps) at post offices and *tabacchi* (look for T signs).

Safety

The crime rate in Italy is generally low, but rates of petty crime higher. Of all the areas mentioned in this book, Stazione Centrale and the metro in Milan are the most likely locations for pickpockets to be operating. Take general care when travelling: don't flaunt your valuables, take only what money you need and split it, and don't take risks you wouldn't at home. Beware of scams and con artists, and don't expect things to go smoothly if you partake in fake goods. Car break-ins are common, so always remove valuables and never leave anything that looks valuable in the car. Take care on public transport where pickpockets or bag-cutters might operate. Do not make it clear which stop you're getting off at – it gives potential thieves a timeframe to work in (most work in groups). Female travellers will find the north of Italy quite safe, apart from some attention from local Lotharios, who are generally harmless.

Telephone

The dialling codes for the main towns in the region are: **Como** 031; **Milan** 02; **Orta San Giulio** 0322; **Stresa** 0323.

You need to use the local codes below even when dialling from within the city or region. The prefix for Italy is +39. You no longer need to drop the initial '0' from area codes when calling from abroad. For directory enquiries call T12.

Time difference

Italy uses Central European Time, GMT+1.

Tipping

Most waiters in the region expect a tip from foreigners; 10-15% is the norm if you're really happy with the service. Leaving change from the bill is appropriate for cheaper *enotecas* and *osterias*. Taxis may add on extra costs for luggage etc but an additional tip is always appreciated. Rounding up prices always goes down well, especially if it means avoiding having to give change – not a favourite Italian habit.

Tourist information
Nearly every town or village has at least 1 tourist information office or booth, while the larger cities boast at least 2 (local and provincial), usually located on the main squares. Most have plenty of information to hand out, as well as having websites, although sometimes these are only in Italian or barely decipherable English. Also check out these helpful websites for more information:

Milan: www.provincia.milano.it.
Italian Tourist Board: www.italian.it.
Bed and Breakfasts in Italy: www.bed-and-breakfast-in-italy.com.

Contents

Milan

When people talk about Italian style, they're really talking about Milanese style – an effortless sense of chic. For those who have even a fleeting interest in fashion, art, design or food, Milan easily sets the heart aflutter. Shopping in Milan – as you would expect – is remarkable. The cuisine is distinctly northern Italian, with restaurants that have to work hard to earn the respect of the discerning locals who obsess over food as much as fashion.

Arriving in Milan

Getting there Trains from all major Italian cities arrive at the **Stazione Centrale** ① *piazza Duca d'Aosta, T892021, www.trenitalia.it*. The **Malpensa Airport Express** (T02-7249 4494) has trains to Stazione Centrale via **Stazione Porta Garibaldi** ① *piazza Sigmund Freud, T892021, www.trenitalia.it*, as well as services to the **Milano Cardorna** ① *Piazzale Cadorna 14, T02-85111*. International, long-distance and some regional buses arrive at the **Stazione Porta Garibaldi** ① *piazza Sigmund Freud, T02-3391 0794*.

Getting around Milan is a great city to walk around, except at the height of summer; however, there is a good public transport system if you need it. The public transport system is run by ① *Azienda Trasporti Milanesi, T800-808181, www.atm-mi.it*, and you can use the same ticket for the buses and trams that crisscross the city. The underground metro system is also effective, if a little tiresome unless you're going at least a few stops. There is an ATM Info Point in the Duomo underground station where you can pick up free route maps. Multi-day passes are available as well. While motor scooters are the most popular way to get around, it's not advisable unless you're used to big city riding, while bicycle riding in Milan is difficult with the tram tracks and cobbled streets.

Tourist information ① *1 Piazza Castello, 1 (corner of Via Beltrami), T02-7740 4343, www. visitamilano.it, Mon-Fri 0900-1800 Sat 0900-1330 and 1400-1800 Sun 0900-1330 and 1400-1700.*

Duomo and centre → For listings, see pages 45-57.

Duomo

① *Piazza del Duomo 18, T02-72023375, www.duomomilano.it. Metro: Duomo. Duomo: daily 0700-1900, free. Treasury: Mon-Fri 0930-1730, Sat 0930-1700, Sun and holidays 1330-1530, €2, tickets at bookshop. Rooftop terrace: Oct-Mar 0900-1900 (last ticket at 1800), Apr-Oct 0900-2130 (last ticket at 2030); €7/3.50 by stairs, €12/6 by lift; tickets at lift entrance. Museum: closed indefinitely for extensive renovations. Information: daily 0900-1200 and 1300-1800. Group bookings, audio guides, books and information are available from Group Welcome Point, set up under the archway of the Church of Santa Maria Annunciata in Camposanto (Piazza Duomo 18, T02-7200 3768). A modest dress code applies, which means covered back, chest and shoulders for women and no shorts for anyone. It's easy to forget in summer, so women should carry a pashmina with them and men wear travel trousers with zip-on/off legs. Wear shoes with grip for the sloped rooftop.*

Milan's main attraction, the monumental Duomo, is indeed something to marvel – dominating piazza del Duomo, it's one of the world's largest cathedrals. But up close it's clear that size isn't all that matters – the fine marble, intricate carvings and exquisite attention to detail are even more impressive. Built on the site of an ancient temple, and facing the public forum, the Duomo remains to this day the city's social and geographical hub, as well as Milan's spiritual centre.

A basilica dedicated to Milan's patron saint, St Ambrose, once stood on the site of the current Duomo as early as the fifth century, but was damaged by fire in 1075. It wasn't until 1386 that Gian Galeazzo Visconti commissioned the current late-Gothic building. More than 300 workers had exclusive use of Candoglia marble, and canals were dredged to bring the stone from Lake Maggiore's quarries. Architects, engineers and artisans came and went and the cathedral was only half-complete when Visconti died in 1402 and construction stalled. Work started and stopped for another four centuries until Napoleon Bonaparte, crowned King of Italy in 1805, ordered that the project be finished, hence the Milanese expression *Fabbrica del Duomo* (meaning 'like the building of the Duomo') to describe a job that takes forever to complete.

Start your tour at the front of the handsome Duomo, facing the mottled pinkish-grey marble façade from the piazza's centre. Here you can best admire its symmetry, elegance and ornamentation: from the beautifully balanced arched windows and towering rows of spires and pinnacles crowned with curlicues, to the 192 statues and 47 bas-reliefs adorning the 3,500 sq m façade. Do a circuit of the Duomo's exterior to more fully appreciate its size and look closely at the thousands of statues decorating the porticoes and set within niches, each a work of art in itself: note the way that material falls and the folds of baby fat on the cherubs. Facing the cathedral, before you enter, admire the bronze panels on the huge doors; started in the mid-1800s they weren't completed until 1966.

Once inside, allow your eyes to adjust to the dimness before exploring these 12,000 sumptuous sq m. Sit awhile to take it all in: the splendid 15th-century stained-glass windows, the 52 columns, and the immense vaulted ceiling. Stroll around, noting the 14th-century tombs of archbishops Ottone Visconti and Giovanni Visconti, and the grisly sarcophagus of St Bartholomew being flayed alive, three splendid altars by Pellegrino Pellegrini, and a Renaissance marble altar embellished with gold statues. Look high above the apse to the dome and the red light bulb: it apparently points to the spot where a nail from Christ's cross was placed. Don't miss the stairs down to the early-Christian baptistery.

Return outside to the rear of the Duomo and take the stairs or elevator to the 70-m high, 8000 sq m roof terrace. Make your way around the roof's perimeter, stopping here and there to better appreciate the wonderful web of flying buttresses, the forest of 135 intricately decorated pinnacles, scores of splendidly carved statues, and enchanting towers with delicate embellishments. Here, the Duomo appears in all its splendour, like something out of a fairytale. Take the stairs to the very top of the roof for marvellous views of Milan framed by Moorish- style arches and soaring steeples. Here you're as close as you're going to get to the gold baroque *Madonnina*, sculpted by Guiseppe Bini, which stands atop the soaring central spire. From her giddy height of 108 m, the little Madonna is said to protect the city.

Galleria Vittorio Emanuele II
① *Piazza del Duomo. Metro: Duomo.*
Once widely known as 'Milan's drawing room', this colossal covered shopping gallery was named after Vittorio Emanuele II, the first king of united Italy, and designed by Giuseppe Mengoni. Built between 1864 and 1878, the splendid double arcade design is in a cruciform

24 hours in Milan

Milan may be a sprawling metropolis but its historic centre is reasonably compact compared to that of Rome or Venice. It's easily explored in 24 hours, although you could add days to visit Milan's world-class museums, see an opera or shop in the fashion quarter. While there are few signs left of ancient Roman *Mediolanum*, there are some marvellous monuments from the Middle Ages and Renaissance, when Milan flourished under the Visconti and Sforza dynasties, like the Duomo and Castello Sforzesco. The periods of French, Spanish and Austrian rule, the Risorgimento and Italian Unification are evident in much of the centre's architecture. This leisurely saunter takes you on a loop from Milan's central square via most of the city's main sights. Do-able in an hour, you could stretch it out to a full day if visiting museums on the way.

Begin your promenade on **piazza del Duomo**, Milan's main square, home to the magnificent **Duomo** (see page 20) and sumptuous shopping arcade **Galleria Vittorio Emanuele II** (see page 21). A public meeting place since Roman times, the piazza is where Milan gathers to celebrate and where tourists and locals alike meet up with friends. To the south

are the grand **Palazzo Arcivescovile** (Archbishop's Palace) and the neoclassical **Palazzo Reale** (see page 22), a museum and venue for contemporary art exhibitions.

Head towards **Galleria Vittorio Emanuele II** (see page 21) to kick-start your walk with a stand-up espresso at the elegant art deco bar at **Zucca in Galleria** (see page 48) with the locals (only tourists sit down) then wander through the galleria, browsing the beautiful window displays before stopping under the central dome to appreciate the mosaics beneath the glass dome, representing each of the continents, and the floor mosaics of the zodiac. Stand in line to stand on Taurus's testicles for good luck, as local custom demands, and watch people get creative with their approaches!

Leave the Galleria by the opposite exit to get to **piazza della Scala**, where you'll find a statue of Leonardo da Vinci. On your right is **Palazzo Marino**, a fine 16th-century residence that has housed Milan's council since 1860. Generally closed to the public, you might be lucky to see an orchestra performing in the interior courtyard, which is used for official functions. To your left is elegant **Teatro alla Scala** (see page 26) where you can pick up an opera

shape leading off piazza del Duomo and ending at piazza della Scala some 196 m away and travelling 105 m on its east-west axis. It was one of the first buildings in Europe to employ iron and glass as structural elements, with its central octagonal space topped with a glass dome 47 m in height. The four floor mosaics around the octagon at the building's centre represent Europe, Africa, Asia and America. You'll see visitors spinning around on one heel under the dome – they're looking for luck by placing their heel on the testicles of a mosaic bull. Luck did not befriend the buildings designer, however… poor Giuseppe Mengoni died from a fall off the roof before the building was completed.

Palazzo Reale

ⓘ *Piazza del Duomo, T02-88465236, Mon 1430-1930, Tue-Sun 0930-1930, Thu 0930-2230, free entry (temporary exhibition fees vary). Metro: Duomo.*

The elegant neoclassical Royal Palace served as the seat of the Milan city council in the 11th century, and as the private residence of the Visconti family from the 12th century. That programme and visit the museum to see the lavish collection of theatre costumes, exquisitely crafted musical instruments, and other opera paraphernalia.

Cross the piazza and veer right – the splendid **Chiesa di San Fedele** will be on your right – and take the tiny lane now to your left, via degli Omenoni, to admire the extraordinary edifice of **Casa degli Omenoni**. Built in 1565, its impressive façade is comprised of colossal carvings of *omenoni* (great men).

At the lane's end, turn left onto via Morone at **Palazzo Belgioioso** where a little further along on your left you'll see **Casa del Manzoni** (see page 26), the restored home of Italy's celebrated author Alessandro Manzoni. At via Alessandro Manzoni, head right to visit the sumptuous **Museo Poldi Pezzoli** (see page 27) or cross Manzoni toward Teatro alla Scala, turning right onto via Giuseppe Verdi for the arty neighbourhood of **Brera** and **via Brera**, lined with contemporary art galleries, design stores, and all kinds of interesting little shops.

When you arrive at the baroque palazzo housing **Pinacoteca di Brera** (see page 36), head inside for a look or turn left onto via Fiori Chiari (and some of Milan's most testing cobblestones!) to explore more of the delightful Brera and its antique stores and coffee shops. Halfway down via Fiori Chiari turn left (where you'll come across a tarot card reader and fortune teller or two) for **piazza del Carmine** and the wonderful **Santa Maria del Carmine** church.

Cross via Mercato, taking another tiny street to busy Foro Bonaparte for the striking **Castello Sforzesco** (see page 30), home to the **Civici Musei** (see page 31) and behind it tranquil **Parco Sempione** (see page 33). Alternatively, turn left to largo Cairoli, then left again on via Dante, a busy commuter corridor and tourist eat street. Once at piazza Cordusio, turn around to admire the Castello views before continuing along this busy pedestrian thoroughfare to the medieval square **piazza Mercanti**, home to the vaulted, red-brick 13th century **Palazzo della Ragione**.

Cross via Mazzini and you're back at piazza del Duomo. If it's late afternoon, amble along via Torino and corso di Porta Ticinese to **Naviglio Grande** for an aperitivo at one of the canalside bars and try the **Navigli Great Night Out** (see page 50).

was until the murder of one of the Viscontis saw the ducal seat moved to the safer address of Castello Sforzesco. The present appearance of the palace is dated to 1778 when it was remodelled as part of a redevelopment of the cathedral square. After extensive restoration in the beginning of this century, the palace is fit for royalty once again, but it essentially serves as a museum and frequently exhibits some highly commended contemporary art, visual design and, occasionally, fashion exhibitions (www.artpalazzoreale.it).

Pinacoteca Ambrosiana
ⓘ *Piazza Pio XI 2, T02-806921, www.ambrosiana.it, Tue-Sun 1000-1800, €10. Metro: Duomo or Cordusio.*

One of Milan's best galleries, the Pinacoteca Ambrosiana's building dates back to 1609 when Cardinal Federico Borromeo introduced it as a public library. The Cardinal's interest in art eventually began to seep into the library and eventually, in 1618, he set up an art gallery here, starting with his own collection of 172 pieces including Titian's *Adoration of*

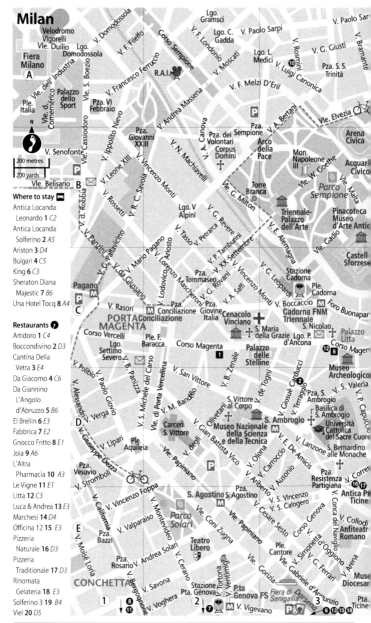

Milan

Where to stay 🛏

Antica Locanda
  Leonardo 1 C2
Antica Locanda
  Solferino 2 A5
Ariston 3 D4
Bulgari 4 C5
King 6 C3
Sheraton Diana
  Majestic 7 B6
Una Hotel Tocq 8 A4

Restaurants 🍴

Artidoro 1 C4
Boccondivino 2 D3
Cantina Della
  Vetra 3 E4
Da Giacomo 4 C6
Da Giannino
  L'Angolo
  d'Abruzzo 5 B6
El Brellin 6 E3
Fabbrica 7 E2
Gnocco Fritto 8 E1
Joia 9 A6
L'Altra
  Pharmacia 10 A3
Le Vigne 11 E1
Litta 12 C3
Luca & Andrea 13 E3
Marchesi 14 D4
Officina 12 15 E3
Pizzeria
  Naturale 16 D3
Pizzeria
  Traditionale 17 D3
Rinomata
  Gelateria 18 E3
Solferino 3 19 B4
Viel 20 D5

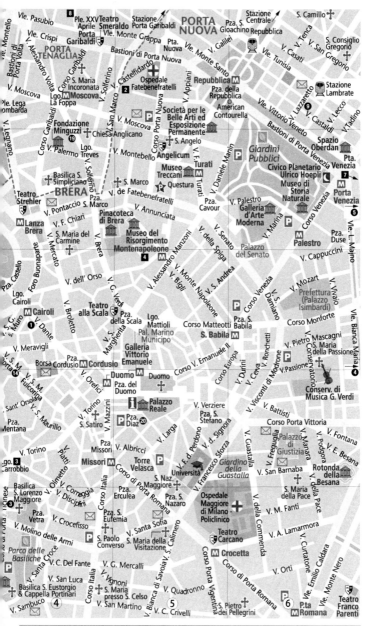

the Magi and Caravaggio's *Canestra di Frutta* (Basket of Fruit) which are both on display. Today there are over 35,000 manuscripts, over 700,000 printed works, some of Leonardo da Vinci's manuscripts, and some excellent paintings in the collection. Notable in the Renaissance collection is Leonardo da Vinci's *Musico* (Musician), while other outstanding painters represented are Botticelli (with the wonderful *Madonna del Padiglione*), Tiepolo and Raphael. There are plenty of curios in the biblioteca but the most interesting are not available for the public to see, including Leonardo da Vinci's 12-volume, bound set of drawings and writings, *Codex Atlanticus*.

Casa del Manzoni

① *Via Morone 1, T02-8646 0403, www.casadelmanzoni.mi.it, Tue-Fri 0900-1200 and 1400-1600, free. Metro: Montenapoleone.*

One of the most stunning things about the home of the great Milanese writer Alessandro Manzoni (1785-1873) is just how perfectly preserved the house is. Manzoni, whose most famous work – *I Promessi Sposi* (The Betrothed) – is an Italian language classic, lived here from 1814 until his death in 1873. The study where he worked features a wonderful painted ceiling.

Teatro alla Scala

① *Piazza della Scala, T02-88791, www.teatroallascala.org. Metro: Duomo. For seating availability and guidelines for purchasing subscriptions and tickets, call Infotel (daily 0900-1800, T02-7200 3744). The easiest way to book from overseas or outside Milan is via the website. In Milan, buy from Central Box Office (Galleria del Sagrato, Duomo metro underpass, beneath piazza del Duomo, performance days 1200-1800). On the day buy tickets from Central Box Office (see above). Or try for one of 140 cheap tickets sold by L'Accordo musical association (1 ticket per person present) at Evening Box Office (via Filodrammatici, La Scala) 2 hrs before performances; only sold to people queuing: for opera/ballet get yourself on the list at 1300 (queue at Central Box Office), for symphony/choir get on the list at 1700 (queue at Evening Box Office), for 7 Dec opening (queue at 1800 6 Dec at Evening Box Office). If you don't make the list, try your luck by showing up – and queuing! – for the leftovers.*

La Scala is one of the most famous opera houses in the world, both for the beauty of the theatre itself and for the history of famous (and infamous) performances and opera debuts – with this elegant theatre the big dramas are not always reserved for the stage! It remains one of the best venues in the world to witness opera and the season-opener is one of the most anticipated events in Milan's, if not Europe's, arts and social calendars. After the major expansions to the theatre, the programme of events runs throughout the year except in August, when most of the city takes a break. The spectacular season opening is on 7 December.

Milan's lavish opera house was inaugurated on 3 August 1778 with Antonio Salieri's opera *L'Europa Riconosciuta*. The name of the theatre came from the church of Santa Maria della Scala which was deconsecrated and demolished to make way for the theatre, now generally just known as 'La Scala'.

While the privileged sat comfortably in their private boxes to enjoy the opera, the main floor of the theatre had no seats (and no orchestra pit) so the less fortunate stood to watch performances. Aficionados who didn't have the connections to score a box seat stood above the boxes in an area called the *loggione*, and the diehard opera fans who still take pride of place here are called the *loggionisti*.

Over the years, countless celebrated performances and premieres have been held at the theatre – alongside many contentious ones. Puccini's 1904 premiere of *Madama Butterfly* was jeered, but the posthumous premiere of his unfinished *Turandot* was moving, the famed conductor Arturo Toscanini putting down the baton and ending the performance where Puccini's notation of the score ended. Even Giuseppe Verdi, the composer whose name is synonymous with La Scala, had his failed openings here. He was at opening night to witness the failure of *Un Giorno di Regno* (1940) whose run was quickly cancelled before success finally came with *Nabucco* (1842). Even Verdi's greatest works were at the mercy of those performing them – *Aïda*, one of the most popular operas in the world, opened the season in 2006 only to have the tenor Roberto Alagna flee the stage during the second night after being booed by the *loggionisti*. His stand-in had to sing the rest of the act in his jeans.

After having just about survived bombing during the Second World War and various renovations, the opera house moved to a new theatre in 2001 while an extensive – and controversial – renovation began. As well as concern over the sensitivity of the planned work on the main opera house, there was concern over the addition of a 'fly tower' – a structure that enables the storage of multiple sets: one of the problems of the old theatre had always been insufficient storage. Despite the controversy, the renovation of the interior was greeted with relief when the theatre and its new museum reopened in 2004.

Museo Teatrale alla Scala
ⓘ *Inside Teatro alla Scala, daily 0900-1230 and 1330-1730 (closed public holidays), €6 museum only, €10 guided tour with booklet (organize directly with official guide Francine Gardino garino@fondazionelascala.it).*
Located inside the opera house, the fabulous museum, restored and reopened in 2004, offers visitors a marvellous insight into La Scala's melodramatic history. While the first floor exhibitions feature lots of fascinating memorabilia and paraphernalia in display cases spread across several rooms, from exquisite antique musical instruments to old opera programmes and photos, the highlight of the exhibition is upstairs in a dramatically lit room of theatrical costumes, many worn by the legendary Maria Callas. Suitable for aficionados and amateurs alike.

Museo Poldi Pezzoli
ⓘ *Via Manzoni 12, T02-796334, www.museopoldipezzoli.it, Tue-Sun 1000-1800, €7/5. Metro: Montenapoleone.*
Art collector Gian Giacomo Poldi Pezzoli was born into an art-loving family and after inheriting the family palace, he began scouring Europe to find elaborate pieces to decorate each room in a different style. On his death, Gian Giacomo, who had no children, stated that he wanted the house and its contents to become a museum, and in 1881 his dying wish was fulfilled. The result is a stunning collection of paintings, tapestries, glass, ceramics, jewellery, clocks, and statues. One of the finest house-museums you'll see anywhere in the world, it's like an antique shop on steroids.

To many art lovers, the key works are the paintings. Gian Giacomo's treasure-trove was never intended to be broadly inclusive, but was meant to be part of a greater collection, helping to illustrate the progress of art in the region, from the Renaissance onwards. Early works in the collection include the painted wooden icon *Madonna dell'Umiltà* by Vitale da Bologna, while the Renaissance period sees plenty of religious paintings. Botticelli is represented by the wonderful *Virgin with Child* and *The Dead Christ Mourned*. Of the 17th and 18th century artists, Giovanni Battista Tiepolo's *Allegory of Strength and Wisdom* is a highlight. From the 19th century, paintings of interest include a portrait of Gian Giacomo Poldi Pezzoli by Francesco Hayez, and a portrait of Giuseppe Poldi Pezzoli by Giuseppe Molteni.

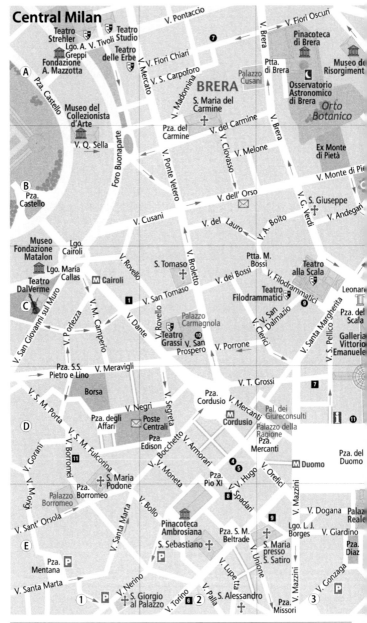

Central Milan

Teatro Strehler
Teatro Studio
Lgo. A. V. Tivoli
Greppi
Fondazione A. Mazzotta
Teatro delle Erbe

V. Pontaccio
V. Fiori Oscuri
V. Brera
Pinacoteca di Brera

V. Fiori Chiari
V. S. Carpoforo
V. Mercato

Museo de Risorgiment

Ptta. di Brera

Palazzo Cusani

BRERA

Museo del Collezionista d'Arte
V. Q. Sella

V. Madonnina
S. Maria del Carmine
Osservatorio Astronomico di Brera
Orto Botanico

Pza. Castello

Pza. del Carmine
V. del Carmine
V. Clivasso
V. Melone
V. Brera

Pza. Castello

Foro Buonaparte
V. Ponte Vetero

Ex Monte di Pietà
V. Monte di Pie

V. dell' Orso
V. G. Verdi
S. Giuseppe
V. Andegar

V. Cusani
V. del Lauro
V. A. Boito

Museo Fondazione Matalon
Lgo. Cairoli
Lgo. Maria Callas

V. Rovello
S. Tomaso
V. Broletto
Ptta. M. Bossi
Teatro alla Scala

Teatro DalVerme

Cairoli
V. San Tomaso
V. dei Bossi
Teatro Filodrammatici
Leonar

V. M. Camperio
V. Dante
V. Rovello
Palazzo Carmagnola
V. San Dalmazio
Pza. del Scala

V. San Giovanni sul Muro
V. Porlezza
Teatro Grassi
V. San Prospero
V. Clerici
V. Porrone
V. Santa Margherita
Galleria Vittorio Emanuele

Pza. S.S. Pietro e Lino
V. Meravigli

V. S. S. Pellico

V. S. M. Porta
Borsa
V. Negri
V. Segreta
Pza. Cordusio
V. T. Grossi
Pal. dei Giureconsulti

V. S. M. Fulcorina
Pza. degli Affari
Poste Centrali
Pza. Edison
V. Bocchetto
V. Armorari
V. Mercanti
Cordusio
Palazzo della Ragione
Pza. Mercanti

V. Corani
V. S. M. Porta
V. Borromei
V. Moneta
Pza. Pio XI
V. Hugo
V. Orefici
Duomo
Pza. del Duomo

Palazzo Borromeo
Pza. Borromeo
S. Maria Podone
V. Bollo
V. Spadari

V. Sant' Orsola
Pinacoteca Ambrosiana
S. Sebastiano
Pza. S. M. Beltrade
S. Maria presso S. Satiro
Lgo. L. J. Borges
V. Dogana
Palaz Reale
V. Giardino
Pza. Diaz

Pza. Mentana
V. Santa Marta
V. Nerino
S. Giorgio al Palazzo
V. Torino
V. Palla
V. Lupetta
V. Unione
S. Alessandro
V. Mazzini
V. Gonzaga

V. Santa Marta
Pza. Missori

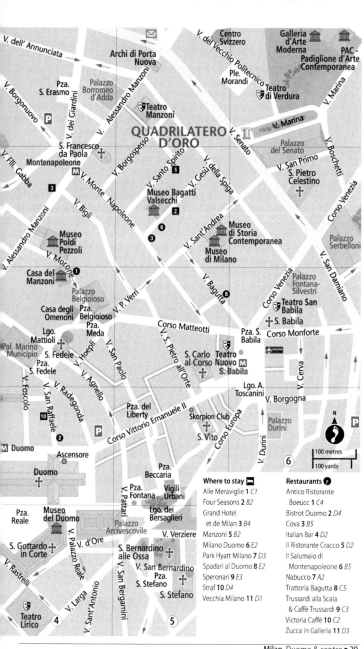

V. dell' Annunciata

Centro Svizzero

Galleria d'Arte Moderna

V. del Vecchio Politecnico

PAC - Padiglione d'Arte Contemporanea

Archi di Porta Nuova

V. Alessandro Manzoni

Ple. Morandi

Teatro di Verdura

V. Marina

Pza. S. Erasmo

Palazzo Borromeo d'Adda

V. Borgonuovo

P

V. dei Giardini

Teatro Manzoni

QUADRILATERO D'ORO

V. Senato

Palazzo del Senato

S. Francesco da Paola

V. Borgospesso

V. Santo Spirito

V. Gesù della Spiga

V. San Primo

S. Pietro Celestino

Montenapoleone

M

V. Monte Napoleone

5

Museo Bagatti Valsecchi

2

Corso Venezia

V. Flli. Gabba

3

V. Bigli

6

V. Sant'Andrea

Museo di Storia Contemporanea

Palazzo Serbelloni

V. Alessandro Manzoni

V. Morone

Museo Poldi Pezzoli

3

Museo di Milano

Palazzo Fontana-Silvestri

Casa del Manzoni

1

V. Bagutta

8

V. San Damiano

Palazzo Belgioioso

Corso Venezia

Teatro San Babila

Casa degli Omenoni

Pza. Belgioioso

Corso Matteotti

S. Babila

Lgo. Mattioli

Pza. Meda

Pza. S. Babila

Corso Monforte

Pal. Marino Municipio

V. Hoepli

V. San Paolo

S. Carlo al Corso

Teatro Nuovo

Pza. S. Fedele

V. S. Pietro all'Ore

S. Babila

M

V. Cerva

V. Foscolo

V. Agnello

Lgo. A. Toscanini

V. Borgogna

V. Radegonda

V. San Raffaele

Pza. del Liberty

Corso Vittorio Emanuele II

Skorpion Club

Palazzo Durini

V. Durini

N

10

2

Corso Europa

S. Vito

P

M Duomo

Ascensore

6

100 metres

100 yards

Duomo

Pza. Beccaria

Pza. Fontana

Vigili Urbani

Duomo

V. Pattari

Lgo. dei Bersaglieri

Pza. Reale

Museo del Duomo

Palazzo Arcivescovile

V. Verziere

V. d'Ore

S. Gottardo in Corte

V. Palazzo Reale

S. Bernardino alle Ossa

V. San Bernardino

V. Rastrelli

V. Larga

V. Sant'Antonio

S. Bernardino Pza. S. Stefano

S. Stefano

Teatro Lirico

4

V. San Bergamini

5

Gian Giacomo Poldi Pezzoli (1822-1879)

Gian Giacomo Poldi Pezzoli's father, Giuseppe, had inherited a fortune from his uncle, including the palace where the museum is now housed. His mother's family, the Trivulzios, had one of the most splendid art collections in Milan, so Gian Giacomo was born into a family where art and beauty were heavily prized.

Following his father's death, when Poldi Pezzoli was only 11, his mother Rosina Trivulzio took charge of his education and continued to nurture his interest in the arts. When he turned 24 in 1846, Poldi Pezzoli was granted access to a considerable fortune, along with the palace. Austrian repression in Lombardy, however, forced Gian Giacomo to take voluntary exile in Europe.

In exile, Gian Giacomo was accumulating knowledge about art collecting, and after being repatriated in 1849, started plans to decorate his personal apartment within the family palace. He methodically collected pieces to suit every room while two of the most noted interior designers of the time, Luigi Scrosati (1815-1869) and Giuseppe Bertini (1825-1898), went to work on the decor. By 1870 the apartment had become famous in art circles. Gian Giacomo Poldi Pezzoli died in 1879, at only 57; in a secretly penned will, he expressed a wish for the house and art to become a museum, and in 1881 his wishes were fulfilled with the museum's opening.

Murano glass fans will love the room dedicated to antique examples of the craft. Armoury was an early collecting favourite of Gian Giacomo Poldi Pezzoli and the results can be seen in the Gallery of Arms. The appropriately named Treasure Chamber is the home of some wonderful jewellery, including ancient Etruscan, Greek and Roman pieces. Ancient works are also represented by the archaeological collection, with some beautiful, if not significant, pieces. The collection of timepieces is significant, on the other hand, with some rare sundials, clocks and watches. The extensive porcelain collection also has some priceless pieces, while the sculptures, fabrics and furniture scattered throughout are worth your while inspecting.

North and west Milan → For listings, see pages 45-57.

Castello Sforzesco
ⓘ *Piazza Castello, T02-88463700, www.milanocastello.it, daily 0700-1800 (winter) and 0700-1900 (summer), admission free for castle grounds. Metro: Cadorna Triennale, Caroli or Lanza.*
Spend a few days in Milan and the majestic red-brick towers of this stately castle, one of Italy's most striking fortifications, will quickly begin to serve as a helpful landmark. If you find yourself approaching the castle from behind, through leafy Parco Sempione, then linger here, or rest up on the manicured lawns of piazza delle Armi within the castle walls – there's a castle to explore and six superb museums to work your way through! But let's start with the castle…

Like the Duomo, Castello Sforzesco has undergone extensive remodelling and renovations over the centuries. Galeazzo II Visconti initiated construction of the first (considerably smaller) defence fortress here on Milan's medieval walls in 1360. The ruins you see to the left of the Filarete Tower are the Porta Vercellina fortifications. His successor Gian Galeazzo strengthened the fortress, while his heir, Filippo Maria, transformed the castle into his own private residence, adding towers to the corners and establishing a big back yard for himself – Parco Sempione. With Filippo Maria's death in 1447, and no direct descendents, Milan was proclaimed a republic and the castle was demolished, its bricks used to rebuild the city walls.

Francesco Sforza married Filippo Maria's illegitimate daughter, Bianca Maria Visconti, three years later and became Duke of Milan. Sforza had a new castle built on the old fortress' foundations with the Filarete tower and round towers. Next in line, Galeazzo Maria built a luxurious residence within the courtyard, the Corte Ducale, and the adjoining fortress within a fortress, the Rocchetta, with the high Torre di Bona. At the end of the late 15th century, Leonardo da Vinci and architect Donato Bramante built a bridge over the outer moat and da Vinci painted the frescoes that are in the Sala delle Asse.

Throughout the sporadic French occupations that spanned nearly 300 years, the castle survived various battles and sackings, until the Filarete tower, being used as ammunition storage at the time, was hit by lightning and exploded. Under Spanish rule in 1526 a star-shaped fortification was constructed around the castle; you'll see this on a number of beautiful illustrations in the museum. Milan's Austrian rulers, who used the castle solely as a military base, strengthened the fortifications over the course of the 18th century, until 1796 when Napoleon's troops arrived to do some damage. Sadly, Napoleon demolished the striking star-shaped structure to better accommodate his troops; the Corte Ducale and da Vinci's beautifully painted Sala stabled the horses!

Following the Unification of Italy in 1861, architect Luca Beltrami reconstructed what was left of the bruised and battered old building so it could be given to the city. In 1905 the splendid new Filarete tower was unveiled and a wonderfully restored fortress was presented to the city for the purpose of housing civic museums.

If you're into museums, you could easily spend a day exploring the castle interiors as you stroll through its many fine exhibitions. If you're simply a fan of castles, then approach the fortress from via Dante, taking in the moats, watchtowers and bulwarks before entering under the stunning Filarete tower. Sprawl out on the grass of the piazza delle Armi with a picnic so you can take in the impressive structures, especially the striking Rochetta, then saunter around the perimeter before resting once again in the shade of a tree in Parco Sempione.

Civici Musei del Castello Sforzesco
① *Castello Sforzesco, piazza Castello, T02-8846 3651/3700, www.milanocastello.it, Tue-Sun 0900-1730 (last admission 1700), €3/1.50, prices for temporary exhibitions vary, free admission on Fri 1400-1730, Tue-Thu and Sat-Sun 1630-1730. Metro: Cadorna Triennale, Caroli or Lanza.*
If exploring the interiors and taking in the architecture of the Castello Sforzesco weren't reason enough to visit these impressive fortifications, inside are half a dozen museums, some of Milan's best, boasting rich collections of archaeology, art, decorative objects and musical instruments. If you're a fan of these, you might want to allocate a couple of days. If you merely want to get an overall impression and focus on the castle itself, you can probably walk through in an hour or so.

Museo Della Preistoria e Protostoria and Museo Egizio   Perhaps start with the Castello's Archaeological Museum, located beneath the Ducal Courtyard. It actually comprises two museums: the Museum of Prehistory and Protohistory and the Egyptian Museum. The former has displays on the Neolithic Age, Bronze Age and Iron Age, while the latter has an admirable collection of ancient Egyptian artefacts, from exhibits on Egyptian writing in the basement rooms to a fascinating collection of mummies, busts of pharaohs and everyday items in the Visconti rooms.

Museo d'Arte Antica On the ground floor of the Ducal Apartments, the Museum of Ancient Art is one of the castle's most impressive museums, with a first-rate collection of sculptures, frescoes, mosaics, stone and terracotta objects, from early Christian times to the 11th century. A highlight is the richly frescoed, wood-panelled Sala delle Asse (room 8), dating to 1498 and decorated by Leonardo da Vinci; unfortunately they've been retouched so many times there's little left of the original trompe l'œil vines. Also worth noting is Michelangelo's unfinished final piece *Rondanini Pietà*, and *Funerary Monument of Gaston de Foix* by Agostino Busti (better known as *Il Bambaja*), both in the Sala degli Scarlioni (room 15). Also in room 15 is *Rondanini Pietà*, a splendid marble sculpture of the Virgin Mary and Jesus which Michelangelo left uncompleted when he died at the age of 89 in 1564.

Upon entering the Sala della Cancelleria (room 1), you'll see the imposing 12th-century marble *Arco della Pusterla dei Fabbri*, a city arch named after the 'posterula', a small back door within one of the medieval city gates. There's a vast collection of Lombard, Roman and Byzantine sculptures from the Early Christian to Middle Ages (from seventh to ninth centuries), including the *Testa di Teodora* (Head of Theodora, the Byzantine Empress) along with splendid fourth century floor mosaics and marble reliefs. Room 2 is crammed with sculptures from Lombardy, particularly Milan, from the Romanesque and Gothic ages, and a huge array of architectural pieces by Lombard artisans such as capitals and decorative shelves found in 12th-century churches in Milan and Pavia, and the Duomo in Cremona. Notable also are Romanesque sculptures from Como and Cremona, and Bonino da Campione's arresting marble *Sepulchral Monument of Bernabò Visconti* on horseback, dating to 1363.

The beautifully lit Sala del Gonfalone (room 7) is worth some time for the room itself and its decorated ceiling; however, the highlights here are rich tapestries, particularly the colourful embroidered silk gonfalon (a banner hung from a crossbar) that depicts the life and miracles of St Ambrose and was consecrated by Milanese cardinal Carlo Borromeo in 1566. In room 14 is *Portale del Banco Mediceo*, an impressive marble portal, dating to 1463, featuring the portraits of Francesco Sforza and Bianca Maria Visconti. Built to seal the Sforza-Visconti alliance, it once stood on via dei Bossi.

Pinacoteca Upstairs, on the first floor of the Ducal Courtyard in rooms 20 to 26, you'll find Milan's most important 'picture gallery'. The Pinacoteca boasts a brilliant collection of some 1,500 paintings, of which 230 are on display, with a wealth of art from the medieval period through to the 18th century, including masterpieces by Mantegna, Canaletto, Antonello da Messina, Tintoretto, Bellotto, Tiepolo, Foppa, Cesare da Sesto, Procaccini, Cerano, and others, along with some important 20th-century pieces by Picasso, Fontana and Sironi. Highlights include several old Milanese collections, such as that of the Trivulzio family. The work is displayed thematically within chronological sequence, with occasional contrasts of genre and period to illustrate the development of different artists and schools of painting. Alongside the paintings are exquisite sculptures, ceramics, terracotta and wooden bas-reliefs.

Museo delle Arti Decorative To get to the Museum of Decorative Arts, follow the stairs leading up from the Ducal Courtyards museums to Ducal Apartments, where the ladies and knights of the Sforza Court once gathered in rooms such as the Sala della Balla. The apartments hold two fabulous museums, the Museum of Musical Instruments (see below), and a museum showcasing a comprehensive collection of furniture, ceramics, majolica tiles, art, precious objects, textiles, jewellery, costumes, armour, and weapons, mostly from Milan and Lombardy, covering the evolution of applied arts from the 15th to the 20th centuries. The pieces are displayed thematically in authentic environments that wonderfully evoke the mood of particular periods, so you can appreciate how fashion has affected taste and lifestyles in Italy, and how different ideas and styles have permeated through various art forms, genres, and even ages. The museum also makes excellent use of multimedia, lighting and interpretative displays to enrich the experience.

The exhibition starts with a display on the 19th-century origins of applied arts and the evolution of 19th and 20th century decorative arts, before returning to the 15th-16th century with 'The Court and the Church' (room 17), the 17th century Chamber of Wonders (room 18), 17th-18th century baroque (room 19), 18th century Collections of the Milanese Nobility (room 16), and the 18th-21st century Masters of Style, from Maggiolini to Sottsass (also in room 16). Don't miss the 14th-16th century frescoes that decorate many of the walls and ceilings, some of which have come from Milanese homes and deconsecrated churches. In room 17, the Chamber of Griselda is a full-scale replica of a room of 15th-century frescoes from Parma's Castello di Roccabianca. A real highlight is the furniture, which features pieces by celebrated designers Ferdinando Bologna, Mario Praz, Alvar Gonzales-Palacios, Peter Thornton and Enrico Colle, and the Masters of Style which illustrates how traditional craftsmanship has evolved in Italy, particularly Milan, through the passing down of skills to an unbroken line of successors, and how this familiarity with historical styles and techniques has resulted in the superlative design that Italians are celebrated for. Make sure you see *Madonna in Glory with Saints* in room 23, one of Mantegna's final pieces. An impressive altarpiece, painted in 1497 for a Veronese church, this was one of his last works. In Sala della Balla are the *Trivulzio Tapestries*, which are named after General Gian Giacomo Trivulzio who commissioned the stunning Tapestries of the Twelve Months, designed by Bramantino in 1503.

Museo degli Strumenti Musicali Remaining upstairs in the Ducal Courtyard museums, you'll find, in what was once a ballroom, one of the finest and largest collections of musical instruments in Europe. A highlight in the Museum of Musical Instruments is the collection of rare violins by Stradivarius, in rooms 36 and 37, and 16th- and 17th-century lutes, guitars, and stringed instruments by the other famous instrument-making families of Cremona: the Amati and the Guarneri. There's also a vast array of wind instruments, including old hunting horns. Gems for the music buffs to seek out include a 16th century Venetian harpsichord, Pietro Verri's rare glass harmonica, Johannes Maria Anciuti's oboe dating to 1722, and Mango Longo's prettily decorated 10-string guitar.

Parco Sempione
ⓘ *Daily 0630-2000 Nov-Feb, till 2100 Mar, Apr and Oct, till 2200 May, till 2300 Jun-Sep. Metro: Cairoli, Cadorna or Lanza.*
This massive park, sprawling behind Castello Sforzesco, is Milan's loveliest green retreat. While the space was only landscaped in its current form in 1894, it was used as a garden and hunting reserve for centuries before. There is lots of shade here, plus waterways, ducks and other birdlife, and plenty of activity in summer when the rest of the city is very quiet – although it's advisable outside of summer to vacate the park before dusk turns to night.

Il Cenacolo (The Last Supper) and Santa Maria delle Grazie

ⓘ *Corso Magenta, T02-8942 1146, www.cenacolovinciano.org. Tue-Sun 0815-1845, closed 1 Jan, 1 May, 25 Dec. Bookings essential. Tickets can be booked online, €6.50 with €1.50 reservation fee. Visits last 15 mins. Metro: Cadorna or Conciliazione.*

Leonardo da Vinci's massive mural that decorates a wall of the Cenacolo Vinciano, the refectory of the Chiesa di Santa Maria delle Grazie, is truly an iconic painting. Much copied, parodied and theorized over, the mural represents the moment when Jesus announces that one of the Twelve Apostles would betray him. Painted between 1495 and 1498, the mural, measuring 880 x 460 cm, has a rich history that almost overshadows seeing the painting in the flesh. Almost.

The church is built in Late Gothic Lombard genre and the nave and two-aisle interior remained traditional in style until 1490, when Ludovico Sforza, a member of Milan's Sforza dynasty, decided to turn the church into his family mausoleum. Ludovico Sforza was an important patron of the arts, and while the artist Donato Montorfano was watching the paint dry on his *Crucifixion* for the refectory in 1494-1495, Leonardo da Vinci was being commissioned by Sforza to adorn the facing wall. Da Vinci decided that the traditional fresco technique – which required that the painting be completed quickly before the wall plaster dried – was unsuited to his style, which involved working in short spurts of inspiration followed by reflection and further embellishment of the work. While Sforza fretted over the time taken, da Vinci was unperturbed, creating sketches and studies, as well as researching painting techniques to fulfil his vision.

Just like the Madonna and Child, the Last Supper was a recurring religious theme for painters. However, da Vinci presented the final gathering of Jesus and his followers in a new style. The Renaissance saw an increasingly realistic portrayal of scenery and people in paintings and da Vinci was an expert at depicting figures in a naturalistic fashion. For instance, while other Last Supper paintings portrayed Judas (the disciple who betrayed Jesus) overtly singled out either with a 'missing' halo or seated apart from Jesus and the other eleven disciples, da Vinci depicts him slightly in the shadows, with an elbow on the table and a small money bag (presumably holding his fee for betraying Jesus) in his hand. Also notable is da Vinci's use of perspective, a relatively new concept at the time, which has the viewer seeing the painting as part of the space of the refectory.

Tickets to see the painting are limited to a certain number a day and entry is carefully controlled, so if you plan to see the painting you must book well in advance. This doesn't mean that you might not get in if you arrive in Milan and spontaneously decide to see it – there's always a chance. But it's best to make sure you don't miss out. You can book online or by phone, but regardless of how you have booked you need to be there at least 20 minutes beforehand to collect the actual tickets – otherwise they may be re-sold. Note that if you've paid by credit card, the cardholder must be present and show identification to collect the tickets.

Leonardo's technique and materials saw the painting deteriorate even in his lifetime. Centuries of poor attempts at restoration, floods and a bombing during the Second World War have all conspired to rob the painting of its impact. The most recent attempt at restoration, which began in 1978 and was completed in 1999, has restored some of the lustre to one of the world's great art treasures.

La Triennale

ⓘ *Viale Alemagna 6, T02-724341, www.triennale.it, Tue-Sun 1030-2030, Thu 1030-2300, €10.*
It's surprising that Milan didn't really have a design museum until 2007, considering the output of cool, contemporary, cutting-edge Italian design over the past century.

Antonio Citterio

While there are many designers of note in Milan, Antonio Citterio, born in 1950, epitomizes what makes Italians so prolific and prominent in the world of design. A graduate of the architecture programme at the Politecnico di Milano in 1972, Citterio has designed everything from lamps to lounge chairs and beds to buildings (such as the Bulgari Hotel, see page 45), and his designs are in the permanent collection of both MoMa (Museum of Modern Art, New York) and the Centre de Pompidou (Paris).

Citterio's work for B&B Italia, Vitra and Kartell furniture companies are wonderful testaments to his skills – and those of Italian designers more generally – combining high-tech research into materials, with comfort, form, and that legendary Milanese style that's understated but still sexy.

As far back as the 1970s Citterio's designs reveal an aesthetic that has continued through to his work today – indeed B&B Italia have a sofa created in 1979 still in production alongside his more recent designs. One of Citterio's greatest skills as a designer is to be able to 'fit' into the style of the firm he has been commissioned by, while still producing distinctive pieces that have his unique mark on them.

The architect's other enviable skill is his ability to design across different disciplines – his studio now handles everything from engineering corporate buildings to creating the graphic identity to go with them. But Citterio's not alone. Many multidisciplinary designers hail from or have worked in Milan, such as the late great Giò Ponte (see box, page 39). Must be something in the acqua…

Fittingly, La Triennale building where the design museum is now housed was originally the Palazzo dell'Arte, built from 1931-1933 for the specific purpose of holding decorative art exhibitions every three years. Today the museum hosts major semi-permanent exhibitions which are installed every 12-18 months, as well as smaller temporary exhibitions, changed every few months.

The striking Palazzo dell'Arte was designed by Giovanni Muzio, who created a massive building that carefully balanced the relationship between external and internal spaces and took advantage of natural light. The architect envisioned the structure as a container in which the interior spaces were flexible – essential for housing exhibitions; however, this was a groundbreaking notion, which made it even more in tune with the purpose of the space.

In 2002, architect Michele De Lucchi overhauled the building, and restored the structure as close as possible to its initial form. In 2007 the building was unveiled to much anticipation, and the Milanese quietly breathed an elegant sigh of relief. The Palazzo dell'Arte had been reinvented in a stunning manner, giving fresh life to the old space while emphasizing the innovative qualities of the early design.

Aptly, the first major exhibition held at the new museum was entitled 'What is Italian Design?' The show highlighted the obsessions of Italian designers, with a special contribution by Welsh film director Peter Greenaway that told the stories of Olivetti (who made business equipment sexy long before Apple) and Vespa (those beloved little motor scooters the Italians ride) amongst others. The inaugural exhibition served to explain how the designs came to be more than purely functional – they became a vital part of Italy's cultural identity. The second major exhibition was on the relationship between art and design – another fitting theme for an outstanding design museum's exploration of Italian innovation.

When you visit, start with the semi-permanent exhibition on at the time, then see the temporary shows, but make sure you leave time to explore the excellent bookshop. Indeed, design junkies might even want a spare hour or two. The hip design café has an open kitchen and, of course, designer chairs and excellent coffee.

Pinacoteca di Brera

ⓘ *Via Brera 28, T02-722631, info line: T02-8942 1146, www.brera.beniculturali.it, Tue-Sun 0830-1915, €6, €5 audio guide. Metro: Lanza or Montenapoleone.*

Located in the lavish 17th-century Palazzo di Brera in the former bohemian quarter, once the atelier of the city's artisans, the sprawling Pinacoteca di Brera boasts one of the most significant collections of Lombard art and a most outstanding collection of Italian and European art from the 13th to 20th centuries – with works by Bellini, Caravaggio, Raphael, Goya, El Greco, Rembrandt and Picasso. Many would argue that if you only see one art museum in Milan, this should be it.

When you visit the pinacoteca one of the first things you'll notice are the art students sketching in front of paintings and hanging out in the courtyards. Most are enrolled at the Accademia di Brera. Established in 1776 it was innovative in its time and remains a prestigious international art school. In 1803, courses were established in architecture, painting, sculpture, engraving, perspective, anatomy and the figure, and in 1805 annual exhibitions of student work were launched which toured Italy and Europe. When the academy's success demanded further expansions, the 14th-century Church of Santa Maria di Brera was demolished. The beautiful sculptures, bas-reliefs, portal and other fragments from the church's façade are in the Museo d'Arte Antica (see page 32) while some of the church's frescoes and paintings are at the pinacoteca itself.

During the Romantic era, under artist Francesco Hayez, the academy led the way in academic painting. The school became highly respected for its art history teaching and, to this day, a place at the academy remains highly prestigious. You'll hear a variety of languages as you pass students chatting in the stairwells – the academy takes 25% of its students from over 50 countries. As a result of the diverse academy, the pinacoteca has a tangible energy and vibrancy about it.

The pinacoteca and collection were established as part of the academy, giving students access to exemplary works of art and sculpture that they could copy and from which they could make plaster casts. The first paintings were acquired during the 'reassignment' of works of art from churches and monasteries under Napoleon Bonaparte's rule, including Raphael's splendid *Sposalizio* (Marriage of the Virgin). Napoleon also sent paintings to the gallery from territories the French army conquered. In 1805, a series of annual art exhibitions was established as a counterpart to the Parisian Salon, and art prizes were introduced, which led Milan to become a centre for fine art throughout the 19th century. After Napoleon III's visit in 1859, a bronze statue of Napoleon I as peacemaker was erected in the courtyard to honour his contribution to the gallery and academy.

The pinacoteca's collection is extensive and exquisite. There are masterpieces from Boccioni, Botticelli, Hayez, Leonardo da Vinci, Tintoretto, Titian, Raphael, Rubens and Modigliani. Highlights include Andrea Mantegna's *The Dead Christ*, which, oddly enough, he painted for his own tomb in Mantua; Mantegna's application of perspective and use of light are exemplary. Gentile Bellini's *St Mark Preaching in Alexandria* is another extraordinary artwork which impresses particularly for its size. At an enormous 347 x 770 cm, it's one of the museum's biggest pieces. The Venetian painter began the painting in 1504, but following his death it was finished by his brother Giovanni Bellini

Milan fashion walk

Fashionistas will want to start early for this spree through Milan's famous **Quadrilatero d'Oro** (Golden Quarter), the city's fashion district, home to glamorous headquarters and flagship stores of exclusive fashion houses. The quadrangle of streets between pedestrianized via della Spiga, via Sant'Andrea, via Montenapoleone and via Manzoni are not only the centre of fashion in Milan, but also a major global fashion hub alongside Paris, New York and London.

Those not so keen on maxing the credit card might consider an evening amble when the streets are quiet and the window displays are even more dramatic; the experience is akin to browsing an illuminated fashion museum. But stroll these smart streets by day and you'll find yourself sharing the cobblestones with brand-obsessed fashion-tourists, stick-thin catwalk models, unflappable fashion designers and their frazzled assistants, and if you're in town during the seasonal fashion weeks, nip'n'tucked celebrities accessorising with bodyguards. The people-watching is half the fun!

Start this walk at **via Manzoni 31**: Emporio Armani. One of Milan's most striking edifices, the statues on the façade of the Assicurazioni Generali building are the patron saints of Milan, Venice and Trieste. Kickstart your stroll with an espresso from **Armani Caffè** on nearby via Croce Rossa.

Continue along via Manzoni, passing design stores Da Driade and Flou, turning right into **via della Spiga**. This cobblestone lane is the quarter's most attractive, boasting some of Milan's best stores, including Sermoneta Gloves, Roberto Cavalli, Moschino, Dolce & Gabbana, Tiffany, Miu Miu, Hermès, Prada, and Bulgari.

At the end, turn right on busy **corso Venezia**, then right onto **via Montenapoleone**, home to Louis Vuitton, La Perla, Ralph Lauren and Gucci. At the corner of **via Sant'Andrea**, stop for refreshments at charming **Cova** (see page 49), a restored tearoom; you might be surprised who you see dropping in for takeaway pastries.

Continue along via Montenapoleone, browsing the alluring windows of Versace, Dior, Pucci, Cartier, Frette, Valentino, Yves Saint Laurent, Ermenegildo Zegna, and Bruno Magli. When you reach **via Manzoni**, backtrack three short blocks and turn left into via Gesù. Call into perfume house Acqua di Parma (see page 55) to inhale their seductive scents and take a look at the lobby of the sumptuous Four Seasons Hotel, accommodation of choice for supermodels and celebrities during Fashion Week.

Turn right onto **via della Spiga**, then right into **via Sant'Andrea**, where you'll find more jaw-dropping window displays at Gianfranco Ferre, Viktor & Rolf, Costume National, Chanel, Kenzo and Trussardi. Turn left into via Bagutta for a meal at one of Milan's most atmospheric eateries, **Trattoria Bagutta** (see page 47).

who, in 1510, painted another masterpiece on show, the *Madonna and Child*. Also look out for Lombard artist Giovanni di Milano, from Caversaccio near Como, and Milanese Gaudenzio Ferrari.

Museo del Risorgimento

ⓘ *Via Borgonuovo 23, T02-8846 4170, www.museodelrisorgimento.mi.it, Tue-Sun 0900-1300 and 1400-1730, free. Metro: San Babila or Montenapoleone.*

The Risorgimento ('Revival') was the political and social movement that led to unification of Italy after Napoleonic rule. The museum, housed in the distinguished Palazzo Moriggia in Brera, has a wealth of Napoleonic memorabilia – including the crown used by Napoleon at his 1805 coronation as King of Italy in Milan. Those with a real bent for history will enjoy the immense collection of Risorgimento manuscripts and documents in the library.

Stazione Centrale
ⓘ *Piazza Duca d'Aosta. Metro: Centrale.*
While most people are too focused on getting out of the station as quickly as possible with their purse or wallet still in their possession (the station is a long-standing pick-pocket paradise), Stazione Centrale is a remarkable and muscular structure. Commissioned in 1912, it wasn't completed until 1931, hence the mix of predominately art nouveau (*stile Liberty* as it was called in Italy) style, smatterings of art deco, and the flamboyant trappings of Fascist-era architecture. Its size is epic, with a 207-m long façade and a height of 70 m, while its enormous glass and iron roof is a thing of beauty. Over 300,000 people pass through the station every day, most of whom would be unaware that binario (platform) 21 has the dubious distinction of being the platform where 600 Jews started their chilling trip to Auschwitz in 1944.

Torre Velasca
ⓘ *Piazza Velasca. Metro: Missori.*
This mischievous medieval-influenced 106-m tower (torre is tower in Spanish, as well as Italian, and the square on which it stands was named after Spanish Governor de Velasca) is a fascinating example of post-war Italian engineering and ingenuity. Built by the firm BBPR, named after the founding architects – Gianluigi Banfi (who was deceased before this building was designed), Lodovico Belgiojoso, Enrico Peressutti, and Ernesto Nathan Rogers – the tower was built between 1956 and 1958. It's unique because of the top nine floors, which are larger and protrude from the floors below, and are supported by buttresses, just like a medieval fortress. One doesn't have to look far to find inspiration for the building – the famous Castello Sforzesco (see page 30) has a very similar form. The mixed-utility building (both residential and office use) was controversial upon its completion, not just because it exploited a loophole in town planning laws, but because of the apparently backward-looking design for the times. Ernesto Nathan Rogers, a well-respected professor of architecture, argued that the shape came organically, once the architects explored what the needs of the building were – and refused to acknowledge that it was based on a medieval tower at all. You can't tour the inside – it's residential and commercial – but it's the exterior architecture that's important.

Pirelli Tower
ⓘ *Piazza Duca d'Aosta. Metro: Centrale.*
When the president of the Pirelli Company (famous for its vehicle tyres, cable manufacturing and girlie calendars) wanted a new skyscraper to be built on the land where their first factory was located, few would have known that he had commissioned what was to be one of the most influential buildings of the second half of the 20th century. Architect Giò Ponti, with the assistance of Pier Luigi Nervi (a master in structures made of reinforced concrete) and Arturo Danusso, designed the building to be a different expression of what a skyscraper could be. Topping out at 127.1 m it is one of the tallest buildings in Milan. An all-concrete construction (most skyscrapers have a skeleton of steel), work started on the building in July 1956, was completed in August 1958, and it opened in 1960. Ponti

Giò Ponte

Giò Ponte (1891–1979) was one of the most influential and important Italian architects of the 20th century, known not just for his creations in cement and steel, but also for his work as a publisher. Ponte studied at the Politechnico di Milano, graduating in 1921, and first earned his reputation working with ceramics. In 1928 he founded the magazine *Domus*, which was to be one of the most influential design magazines in the world, which he edited (apart from a break between 1941-1948) until his death. In addition, Ponte was also an academic and was a professor in the Faculty of Architecture at the Politechnico di Milano from 1936 to 1961.

Throughout his career, this leading light of modern Italian design created many objects that are seen as classics today. Chairs and sofas, for instance, were one area where he left his modernist mark. Ponti had a light touch, best demonstrated by his famous *Superleggera* chair (1957), which he spent ten years perfecting in an attempt to find the right balance between lightness and strength – hence the name 'superlight'. The chair – able to be lifted with one finger by a child – is still manufactured by Cassina furniture in Italy today. Another example of his great multidisciplinary work is the La Cornuta Mod 47 espresso machine designed in 1948 for La Pavoni (inventors of the first espresso machine in 1905), which appears more on museum shelves than in cafés these days. However, it is the hexagonal-based Pirelli Tower in Milan that Ponti is mostly remembered for, although those with only a passing interest in architecture would be hard-pressed to see the significance of it. But this is exactly what *is* significant about architects such as Ponti – until the Pirelli Tower, most skyscrapers were simply boring rectangular blocks.

saw the unusual diamond shape as a 'graphic slogan', being somewhat obsessed with the diamond form during the 1950s. Also known as 'Pirellione' (or Big Pirelli), today it's home to the Lombardy regional government – which had an unexpected tragedy on 18 April 2002 when a light plane unintentionally crashed into the building, killing the pilot and two office workers. The building structure remained intact and was repaired and still stands as testament to the prosperous and creative post-war era of Italy. Although you can only enter the lobby, one of the best uninterrupted views of the tower is from the piazza just in front of Stazione Centrale – just watch out for pickpockets…

East Milan → *For listings, see pages 45-57.*

Museo Bagatti Valsecchi

ⓘ *Via Gesù 5, T02-7600 6132, www.museobagattivalsecchi.org, Tue-Sun 1300-1745, €8.*
Housed in Palazzo Bagatti Valsecchi, this museum was the home of brothers Fausto and Giuseppe Bagatti Valsecchi who filled – and we mean filled – this 19th-century mansion with exquisite art, furniture and other beautiful objects dating back to the Renaissance era. It's a sumptuous dwelling that's every bit as intriguing as the two brothers intended to make it.

Museo di Milano

ⓘ *Palazzo Morando Attendolo Bolognini, via Sant'Andrea 6, T02-8846 5933, www.museo distoriacontemporanea.it, Tue-Sun 1400-1730, free. Metro San Babila or Montenapoleone.*

One for the museum buffs and scholars of art, this compelling museum is home to a fastidious collection of documents and paintings related to the history of Milan, particularly from Napoleonic times through Austrian rule. Exquisitely renovated, the 18th-century Palazzo Morando Attendolo Bolognini is also a living museum showing the apartments of Countess Bolognini and their beautiful objects. The building also houses the Museo di Storia Contemporanea (see below).

Museo di Storia Contemporanea

ⓘ *Palazzo Morando Attendolo Bolognini, via Sant'Andrea 6, T02-8846 5933, www.museo distoriacontemporanea.it. Tue-Sun 1400-1730, free.*

Housed in the same lovely, restored palazzo as the Museo di Milano (see above), the fascinating Museum of Contemporary History looks at the more recent development of the city, and in particular how it has culturally and geographically expanded, with an emphasis on changes following unification, and particularly around the two World Wars.

Museo dell'Ottocento

ⓘ *Villa Barbiano di Belgiojoso (formerly known as Villa Reale), via Palestro 16, T02-7600 2819, Tue-Sun 0900-1300 and 1400-1730, free. Metro: Palestro.*

The 'Museum of the 1800s' is appropriately located in the elegant, neoclassical Villa Barbiano di Belgiojoso, built in 1790 for Count Ludovico Barbiano di Belgiojoso, but better known as the residence of the King of Naples Gioacchino Murat and his wife (Napoleon's sister) Carolina Bonaparte, during the early 1800s. The collection of the renovated and re-focused former Galleria d'Arte Moderna (Gallery of Modern Art) is spread throughout 35 rooms and features Italian and European neoclassical art (ground floor), art from the Romantic period, the Milanese Scapigliatura movement, Post-Impressionist Divisionism and Futurism (first floor), and the Grassi and Vismara collections of Italian and international modern art, which include work by masters such as Gaugin, Matisse and Picasso (second floor). Even after renovation, it seems there still isn't enough room to show all 2,700 paintings and sculptures from the Gallery of Modern Art, and part of the collection has moved to another museum, the **Museo del Novecento** ⓘ *via Marconi 1, T02-8844 4061, www.museodelnovecento.org, Mon 1430-1930, Tue, Wed, Fri, Sun 0930-1930, Thu and Sat 0930-2230, €5/€3.* The villa's romantic English-style gardens boast beautiful bas-reliefs and statues of mythological subjects and are worth a wander; guided tours are also offered.

Padiglione d'Arte Contemporanea

ⓘ *Via Palestro 14, T02-7600 9085, www.comune.milano.it/pac, Mon 1430-1930 Tue-Sun 0930-1930, Thu 0930-2230 (opening hours can vary according to exhibitions). Metro: Palestro.*

Adjoining the Galleria d'Arte Moderna, this cutting-edge contemporary art gallery hosts temporary exhibitions that are almost always engaging and often provocative. The building's history is equally compelling. Built in 1947 as a symbolic post-war gesture to replace the Villa Belgiojoso, which had been destroyed by bombing, it was closed in the 1970s and renovated and reopened a decade later with new aims, only to be bombed again by the mafia in 1993! On re-opening, the museum was each time determined to become significantly more pro-active. This guiding principle persists today, particularly through its art education programme and artistic teaching laboratory for the visually impaired. The building itself is used to teach art, enabling students to interact with the building's structure and surfaces as well as the art. There's a good bookshop, cafeteria and video room.

Giardini Pubblici
ⓘ *0630-dusk. Metro: Palestro.*

These elaborate public gardens were built in the mannered English style. Designed in 1784 by Giuseppe Piermarini, they are the largest gardens in the city centre, providing relief from the inner city and the suburbs of Milan. Piermarini also designed Teatro alla Scala (see page 26) and corso di Porta Romana, the first paved street of modern Europe. Museums and galleries ring the park and it's a good one for joggers – just watch the dogs! Children who aren't obsessed with portable video games will get a kick out of the old-fashioned amusements at the park's western end. The natural history museum, planetarium and film museum are all located in the Giardini Pubblici.

Museo Civico di Storia Naturale
ⓘ *Corso Venezia 55, Giardini Pubblici, T02-8846 3280, Tue-Sun 0900-1730, €3/free. Metro: Porta Venezia or Palestro.*

The Museum of Natural History is housed in a handsome terracotta neoclassical building dating to 1838. It was constructed mainly to house the collection left to the city by Giuseppe de Cristoforis and the exhibits cover botany, geology, mineralogy, palaeontology and zoology, which essentially translates to plenty of old-fashioned fun, stuffed animals and strange rocks. The dioramas of animal habitats are a treat as are the life-size dinosaur skeletons.

Planetario Ulrico Hoepli
ⓘ *Corso Venezia 57, Giardini Pubblici, T02-8846 3340, public viewing sessions Tue and Thu 2100, €3/1.50. Metro: Porta Venezia or Palestro.*

Donated to the city by the publisher Ulrico Hoepli, the Planetario was designed by Pietro Portaluppi in 1930 and is still the biggest public planetarium in Italy. During viewing sessions, a film of the celestial seasonal positions is projected onto the dome of the planetarium.

Museo del Cinema
ⓘ *Palazzo Dugnani, via Daniele Manin 2, Giardini Pubblici, T02-87242114, www.cineteca milano.it, Thu-Sun 1500-1900, €3. Metro: Turati, Porta Venezia or Palestro.*

Located on the west side of the park, this cinema museum, housed in the restored 17th-century Palazzo Dugnani, is an intimate one. Film geeks will love the equipment from the early years of cinema, such as hand-wound cameras and sound equipment, as well as some wonderful retro film posters. The museum has screenings of Italian film classics as well; see the website for screening details.

South Milan → *For listings, see pages 45-57.*

Museo Nazionale della Scienza e della Tecnica Leonardo da Vinci
ⓘ *Via San Vittore 21, T02-485551, www.museoscienza.org, Tue-Fri 0930-1700, Sat and Sun 0930-1830, €10/7.*

Housed in a former 16th-century monastery, the Leonardo da Vinci National Museum of Science and Technology is a must for fans of da Vinci and science geeks. Tracing the history of technology and science in an engaging fashion is the aim of this educational museum and while it will expand your mind, the drawings coming from the mind of one of the most talented human beings ever to walk the earth – Leonardo da Vinci – are quite extraordinary.

Leonardo da Vinci

When you stand in front of one of the most significant paintings in the world, *The Last Supper* (see page 34), it's hard to believe that the same man who painted it was also the first known person to conceptualize the helicopter.

Leonardo da Vinci (1452-1519) might not have built a prototype of the flying machine, but he was the prototype of what was to be named a 'Renaissance man', with an unquenchable thirst for knowledge of science, nature and the arts. This quest for knowledge was complemented by his abilities as an inventor. However, many of his sketches would only come to life hundreds of years after his death.

While alive, Leonardo da Vinci had his mysteries. An illegitimate child, he was never married nor had children. Instead, he devoted himself to mentoring others. While his extraordinary talents in such diverse fields have seen him labelled perhaps the greatest genius of mankind, it was his talent as a painter that has earned him his place amongst the greatest artists to ever live.

Both *The Last Supper* and the *Mona Lisa* are more than just paintings – their iconic status has seen these works of art widely copied and parodied. Ironically, it was da Vinci's own experimentation and restlessness that led us to have so few of his works surviving today. Painted in 1498, *The Last Supper* was already showing serious signs of deterioration by the mid 1500s, due to da Vinci's experiment with the technique of tempera – mixing pigment with egg. See also page 34.

There are six different easy-to-navigate areas of the museum, dedicated to the history of science and technology – Materials, Energy, Transport, Communication, New Frontiers, and Leonardo, Art and Science – but prepare yourself for an overwhelming 10,000 objects in the collection. Fortunately, there are interactive guides and stations to explain many of them, and one of the highlights for children (of all ages!) is the iLabs – 15 interactive laboratories.

In the Materials area you can learn how paper, metal and plastic are processed for use, and look at the techniques used to manufacture them in the 'iLab'. The Energies area looks at how energy is harvested and distributed, and includes the wonderful Regina Margherita, an elegant thermoelectric power plant that still functions. The Transport section is one of the most visual of the museum, with a full-size submarine that you can board, the *Enrico Toti*, built in 1967, and put out of service in 1999. Other exhibits include trains, ships, aeroplanes and helicopters. In the Communication section everything is covered from Gutenberg's movable type machine to mobile phones, with a look at graphic art and sound as well. The New Frontiers section explores the worlds of biotechnologies, genetics and robotics, and takes a peek into the future. Looking back to one of the greatest minds of history is the Leonardo Gallery, where outstanding models have been made of the great thinker's sketches, vividly bringing them to life, while the Art and Science section (something that da Vinci had no problem combining) looks at how art and technology have a symbiotic relationship.

Weekends and public holidays might be crowded at the museum, but there are more activities scheduled, including guided tours and plenty of interactive learning experiences taking place. This is definitely one place where children will have a great time, so allow for at least a couple of hours – even more if they're scientifically inquisitive.

Basilica di Sant'Ambrogio

① *Piazza Sant'Ambrogio 15, T02-8645 0895, www.basilicasantambrogio.it, Mon-Sat 1000-1200 and 1430-1800, Sun 1500-1900, free. Metro: Sant'Ambrogio.*

Bishop Ambrogio (Ambrose is the anglicized form), the patron saint of Milan, commissioned this fascinating basilica which was constructed between AD 379-386, and built over a cemetery that held the bodies of two Christian martyrs. Since then it has been rebuilt several times, resulting in the assortment of styles that is present today, which explains the mismatched bell towers – the shorter being built in the ninth century, the taller in 1124. Inside, the ciborium (the freestanding canopy over the altar) is notable, as is the golden altar housing the remains of St Ambrose, and dating to the ninth century. It features reliefs of the life of Jesus on the front and the life of the saint on the back.

Chiesa di San Lorenzo Maggiore

① *Piazza Vetra, corso di Porta Ticinese 39, daily 0730-1230 and 1430-1830, free. Metro: Missori.*

This church is one of the first Christian churches built, dating to AD 355-372. It was commissioned by Bishop Ambrose and renovated in the 13th century, its large dome rebuilt in 1573. Outside the church, the statue in the piazza is a copy of one of Emperor Constantine, who allowed Christianity to be practised with the Edict of Milan in AD 313. Also here are Milan's most beloved Roman remnants – a row of 9-m-tall columns that were part of a third-century temple moved here in the fifth century. The piazza remains one of Milan's favourite meeting spots and locals like to sit at the base of the columns and enjoy a cold beer on balmy summer evenings.

Sant'Eustorgio

① *Piazza Sant'Eustorgio, daily 0730-1200 and 1530-1830, free. Metro: Missori or Porta Genova.*

Another one of Milan's churches featuring a medley of styles, the origins of this one date back to the seventh century. It was updated in the ninth century, and once again altered in the 11th, with more modifications up to the 15th before it was topped by a neo-Romanesque façade in 1865. The highlights of the church are the *Cappella Portinari* (Chapel of St Peter Martyr) built between 1462 and 1466, and the frescoes by Renaissance painter Vincenzo Foppa.

Certosa di Pavia → *For listings, see pages 45-57.*

① *Viale Certosa, Pavia, www.certosadipavia.com. Church and grounds daily 0900-1700; certosa (including cloister and shop) Tue-Sun 0900-1130 and 1430-1730, free. Certosa di Pavia is 30 km south of Milan and 10 km north of Pavia. If driving from Milan, take the SS35 to Pavia, then turn left at viale Certosa. Buses from Milan leave from Milan Famogasta metro station (€3), dropping you a 15-min walk from the certosa; tell the driver where you are going so they can alert you when to hop off. Remember to dress modestly.*

An easy half-hour ride from Milan, the exuberant Certosa di Pavia (Charterhouse of Pavia) is an enchanting place to while away a day. Built between 1396 and 1465, this splendid Carthusian monastery complex has a fairytale Gothic church with an extravagant façade and elaborate interior. The elegant palace has graceful gardens to stroll through as you contemplate (in silence of course!) the stark contrast between the monks' simple life of confinement and the lavish riches on show within the church.

Located at the end of a shaded lane and set in velvety parkland that was once the Visconti dynasty's hunting park, the place is perfect for a picnic. You'll have to bring your own hamper as there's nowhere to purchase anything nearby, though you can buy dessert here – the monk's home-made chocolate from the monastery shop.

Home to the Carthusian monastic order, Certosa di Pavia is the finest Carthusian monastery in Italy: there is no match when it comes to sheer architectural grandeur, opulent detail and the extraordinary riches on display inside. Commissioned by Gian Galeazzo Visconti, the magnificent church and monastery were principally built to house the Visconti dynasty mausoleum. Indeed, the location was a strategic choice – part way between Milan and the duchy's second city, Pavia, where the Duke kept his court.

Inspired by Milan's Duomo (see page 20), the richly ornamented church façade is a model of symmetrical perfection. Adorned with inlaid marble, intricately carved statues, buttresses, and bas-reliefs that tell the history of the *certosa*, it boasts a beautiful classical arched portal with Corinthian columns, a large central window, and elegant rows of shallow arched balconies. What makes the church so impressive, though, is its truly monumental interior, which is modelled on the Latin cross plan, with a colossal nave, two aisles and transept. The glorious vaulted ceiling is supported by Gothic arches and decorated with a starry sky. Throughout the main chapel and its adjoining enormous chapels are marble altars, wooden choir stalls, beautiful bronze candelabra and ivory triptychs.

If that wasn't enough, the whole church is decorated with a wealth of art. Required to spend revenue from the lands to improve the building, the monks gradually amassed enormous collections of riches with particularly impressive artworks from the 15th and 18th centuries. Expect to see wonderful frescoes, paintings and panels by Bergognone, Giovanni Battista Crespi and Guercino, sculptures by Giovanni Antonio Amadeo and the Mantegazza brothers, and stained glass windows by some of Lombard's finest 15th-century artists, including Bergognone, as well as Zanetto Bugatto and Vincenzo Foppa. The tomb of Gian Galeazzo Visconti is in the southern transept while that of dynastic rival Ludovico Sforza and his wife Beatrice d'Este is in the northern transept.

After you've lingered in the church awhile, exit through the elegant portal at the rear (a monk is usually there to show you the way), which leads to the Small Cloister with a pretty garden at its centre and arcades decorated with frescoes. From here you can peek into the Grand Cloister, where the monks' cells open onto the main garden. In this cloister the columned arcades are prettily decorated in pink and white marble with saints, prophets and angels. Take a leisurely amble around the perimeter of the small cloister; from the southern side you can enjoy a lovely vista across the gardens to the church, which is the real highlight for some.

Time spent at the *certosa* is really a wonderful assault upon the senses, so allow lots of it. Before you leave, drop by the shop where you can buy Chartreuse liqueur and chocolate made by the monks alongside herbs grown in the gardens and aromatic soaps.

If you have your own wheels, then Pavia is worth a quick look. Once one of northern Italy's most powerful cities, the town has a pleasant medieval *centro storico*, and the Università degli Studi di Pavia is one of Europe's oldest.

Milan listings

For hotel and restaurant price codes and other relevant information, see pages 10-13.

🛏 Where to stay

Self-catering

€€€-€ RentXpress, www.rentxpress.com. RentXpress offers a virtual phonebook full of apartments across Milan that are fantastic value if you're staying more than a few nights. Many of them boast chic decor and most are fully equipped for self-catering. Some are in superb locations, such as the waterfront apartments in the Navigli; however, some are inconveniently located for sightseeing.

€€-€ Milan Apartment Rental, T02-950 5689, www.milanapartmentrental.it. While amenities vary, generally these apartments are elegant and stylish, fully furnished, and fully equipped for self-catering. All have Wi-Fi, satellite TV and DVD player, and bed linen and towels. As with any of these kinds of properties, location is king, so make sure the apartment is in a good area for living like a local.

€ Friendly Home, T02-8691 0453, www.friendly-home.org. An organization offering a range of B&Bs and studios (suitable for self-catering) for short stays in Milan. Some are situated in historic houses, while others are of the modern Milanese style. As they have properties all over, make sure you choose according to your itinerary.

Duomo and centre *p20,*
maps p24 and p28

€€€ Park Hyatt Milano, Via Tommaso Grossi 1, T02-8821 1234, www.milan.park. hyatt.com. The unbeatable position (Duomo, Galleria and La Scala just steps away) would be enough to make this hotel popular, but the service and attention to detail are what really sets it apart. The rooms are sizeable, with plush carpets, every imaginable amenity, and large

Italian marble-clad bathrooms. The hotel's restaurant is excellent.

€€€ Spadari al Duomo, Via Spadari 11, T02-7200 2371, www.spadarihotel.com. A small design hotel that has oodles of real personality is rare, but the Spadari has it in spades. Each room is well-appointed and cosy, personalized by Italian artists, but it's the staff and service that really make this small hotel something quite special. A fantastic location just 1 block from the Duomo and right next door to the best delicatessen in Italy, Peck (see page 56), makes it a tempting option.

€€€-€€ Straf, Via San Raffaele 3, T02-805081, www.straf.it. Since the Straf's opening, guests' responses to it have been mixed to say the least. Some love the design (cement walls, black stone, burnished brass and low-key lighting) while others appear to have been distressed by the experience of the womb-like rooms. We've only been slightly traumatized by the service, which is hit and miss, but we love the aperitivo scene, the good breakfast and the great location.

€ Speronari, Via Speronari 4, T02-8646 1125. The best of the budget picks has an unbeatable location in an atmospheric area near the Duomo. Basic rooms can be booked with or without bathroom (the former are much better) and rooms facing the courtyard are quieter than street-facing rooms. The hotel might not be as interesting as the streets around it, but in this category in this fantastic location, it's slim pickings.

North Milan *p30*

€€€ Bulgari, Via Privata Fratelli Gabba 7/b, T02-805 8051, www.bulgarihotels.com. Exclusive and exquisite with lovely gardens, this hotel designed by renowned Antonio Citterio is quite the oasis of cool. Unlike other 'boutique' style properties in Milan, the staff are helpful and the fantastic spa is worthy of a serious set of treatments. Rooms are generous in size and the bar and restaurant •

exemplary, so it's actually hard to leave the premises and face the 'real' Milan outside.

€€€ Four Seasons, Via Gesù 81, T02-77088, www.fourseasons.com. There's nothing austere about this elegant former 15th-century monastery right in the heart of the shopping district. Unapologetically lavish and with service that lifts this **Four Seasons** above the pack, it's *the* address to put your bags down in after a serious shopping excursion. Unless you're in one of the spacious suites, you might find the rooms a tight squeeze.

€€€ Grand Hotel et de Milan, Via Alessandro Manzoni 29, T02-723141, www.grandhoteletdemilan.it. This is Milan's opera-lovers' hotel of choice, not only for the proximity to the famous **La Scala**, but for the fact that it was once home to composer Giuseppe Verdi. Originally opened in 1863, the opulent furnishings in the rooms reflect the different eras of the hotel's life. Staying in the Verdi suite and eating at the fabulous **Don Carlos** restaurant makes for a memorable night in.

€€€ Manzoni, Via Santo Spirito 20, T02-7600 5700, www.hotelmanzoni.com. The **Manzoni** is in an enviable shopping district location (between the 2 best shopping streets in the city). It's also a sumptuous property, with plenty of marble and fancy furnishings. With LCD TVs, Wi-Fi and all other mod cons, it's an excellent value 4-star, so upgrade to a suite before the prices inevitably rise.

€€ Antica Locanda Solferino, Via Castelfidardo 2, T02-657 0129, www.anticalocandasolferino.it. This comfortable, personal *locanda* has 11 individually decorated rooms with lovely engravings and fascinating antique pieces. Its charm lies in its idiosyncratic and arty nature, so those wanting to tick off amenities lists should look elsewhere. The Brera is a great area to stay in, with plenty of restaurants and shopping.

€€ Una Hotel Tocq, Via A De Tocqueville 7d, T02-62071, www.unahotels.it. The Italian **Una** group has a number of hotels in the city, but this one is best positioned (in the heart of corso Como) if you're in town for shopping, bars and clubs. While the design isn't as fashionable as it once might have been, the rooms are a decent size and have a good level of amenities.

West Milan p30

€€ Antica Locanda Leonardo, Corso Magenta 78, T02-4801 4197, www.anticalocandaleonardo.com. This small, family-run hotel is for those who dislike the anodyne experience of a chain hotel. Room styles vary, but all have a/c, Wi-Fi and satellite TV. The bonus comes with the service, with the staff happy to make bookings for you at recommended restaurants and get tickets for the must-do *Il Cenacolo* (The Last Supper).

€ Alle Meraviglie, Via San Tomaso 8, T02-805 1023, www.allemeraviglie.it. A small B&B done up in a style your grandmother would probably like, it's a simple, charming place that provides respite from the busy streets of Milan. Everything here is fresh, light and floral, and while amenities are thin on the ground it's all about the atmosphere – for better or worse, depending on your needs.

€ King, Corso Magenta 19, T02-874432, www.hotelkingmilano.com. The 'King Mokinba', as it's fondly known, offers up decent and endearingly old-fashioned digs. The rooms do vary in size (so be persistent in asking for a larger room), all are spotless, and the amenities level is good. Good location, with bars close by and the convenience of Cadorna and the Malpensa Express (for the airport) a short distance away.

East Milan p39

€€€ Sheraton Diana Majestic, Viale Piave 42, T02-20581, www.starwoodhotels.com. This wonderful Liberty-style building is home to a hotel with a dual personality – the charming and welcoming set of 107 rooms and suites with original furniture (and wonderful beds) is offset by the chic aperitivo scene that is unrivalled in Milan. A great address in a city where guests can otherwise be treated a little offhandedly. There's a fine restaurant too, if you can't be bothered with leaving the hotel after aperitivo.

€€ SouthHotel Ariston, Largo Carrobbio 2, T02-7200 0556, www.aristonhotel.com. The Ariston is a decent 3-star hotel that's well positioned for the sights, shopping and nightlife. Room sizes vary; there are some spacious doubles (the deluxe rooms on the 8th floor are recommended), but some singles are only fit for a monk. The hotel has pretensions to being an ecological hotel with 'bioarchitecture', but there's little evidence of it. There is, however, very handy on-site parking.

€ Bed & Breakfast Milano Duomo, Via Torino 46, T347-779 6170, www.bbmilano duomo.it. A welcome addition to the property-starved B&B scene, the location (right near the Duomo on a busy shopping street) make it a good choice. Bright and comfortable, the rooms are relatively generous in size and spotlessly clean. The staff take pride in knowing where to send guests to dine. No credit cards.

€ Vecchia Milano, Via Borromei 4, T02-875042, www.hotelvecchiamilano.it. A small and very modest 27-room hotel, it has the feel of a B&B rather than a fully fledged hotel. All rooms have a/c (sometimes they don't in this price range) and are simply decorated. Friendly staff and handily placed for shopping and local restaurants.

🍴 Restaurants

Duomo and centre *p20,*
maps p24 and p28
€€ Antico Ristorante Boeucc, Piazza Belgioioso 2, T02-7602 0224. Closed Sun and Mon lunch and Aug. This timeless restaurant, elegantly housed in an 18th-century *palazzo*, reflects the clientele of bankers and businesspeople – they want reliable, unsurprising food offering a good return for their investment. **Boeucc** delivers

with refined versions of Milanese classics such as *ossobucco*.

€€ Bistrot Duomo, Via San Raffaele 2, T02-877120. Closed Sun and Mon lunch and Aug. If you can take your attention away from the dramatic views of the Duomo from the top floor of **La Rinascente** department store building, this refined restaurant serves up regional classics. You can't go wrong with this good mix of views, cuisine, service and a decent wine list.

€€ Il Ristorante Cracco, Via Victor Hugo 4, T02-876774. Closed Sat and Sun lunch and Aug. Carlo Cracco is Milan's mad-scientist chef, his experimentation has earned him a place amongst the best chefs in the world and the elegant confines of his restaurant belie the wildness of his vivid imagination. While foodies flock here, less adventurous or informed diners might baulk at some of the creations.

€€ Il Salumaio di Montenapoleone, Via Montenapoleone, T02-7600 1123. Closed Sat and Sun lunch. Along with **Trattoria Bagutta** (below), this small, enticing courtyard restaurant, fronting their excellent delicatessen, knows how to refuel patrons in the middle of a shopping expedition. If you think the filled tortellini might see you go up a size, don't dare peruse the dessert menu.

€€ Italian Bar, Via Cesare Cantù 3, T02-869 3017. Closed Sun. This smart, no-nonsense restaurant (part of the Peck delicatessen empire) has locals so loyal the waiters can punch in their order from memory. While others might struggle to actually get a waiter's attention, it's worth persevering for the quality and simplicity of the cuisine. Good short wine list.

€€ Trattoria Bagutta, Via Bagutta 14-16, T02-7600 2767. Closed Sun. Don't be put off by the dark entrance – seating out the back, in or adjoining the courtyard, are *primo* positions for lunch. Calorie-counters pick at the first-rate antipasto bar while everyone else lets the old-school atmosphere take over and orders staples such as *ossobucco*.

Eating out in Milan

Milan is great for foodies, boasting some of Italy's finest gastronomic experiences at the best restaurants. It can also be a really fun city to eat in, with countless casual *trattorias*, *osterias* and *enotecas* offering an easy and quick no-nonsense meal – or a slow one if you prefer it! Always check in advance to make sure your restaurant of choice is open, as owners have been known to close on a whim – if there's a big football match on, for instance, or the weather is particularly bad. Generally, most restaurants and trattorias open for lunch (1200-1500) and dinner (1900-2300) at least six days and nights a week, although some of the finest restaurants might only open for dinner. *Osterias* and *enotecas* won't often open until late afternoon, but will stay open serving food later than restaurants. The best restaurants close for August, when the locals head to the beaches and Milan becomes a ghost town; they might also close for a couple of weeks in January, after Christmas and New Year, so it's best to book your Michelin-starred restaurants well in advance.

€€ **Trussardi alla Scala**, Piazza della Scala 5, T02-8068 8201. Closed Sat and Sun lunch. Chef Andrea Berton's dishes are a delight, with comforting classics such as risotto uplifted with sweetbreads. There's a brilliant cellar and a surprisingly relaxed atmosphere considering it's a Michelin-starred restaurant.

Cafés

Café Trussardi, Piazza della Scala 5, T02-8068 8295. This stylish café and bar opposite La Scala is a local favourite because you can get everything here from panini in the morning or an excellent quick lunch to aperitivo hour drinks and prosecco during the opera's intermission.

Victoria Caffè, Via Clerici 1, T02-805 3598. This sumptuous café hosts a parade of Milan's financiers who re-energize with coffee during the day and something stronger after the markets close. Great aperitivo snacks.

Zucca in Galleria, Galleria Vittorio Emanuele II 21, T02-8646 4435. Milan's must-do café is a stand-up caffeine-shot-stop for the locals, while visitors dominate the outside seating. Check out the lovely art deco interior.

North Milan *p30*

€€ **Artidoro**, Via Camperio 15, T02-805 7386. Closed Sun. A neighbourhood favourite, this *osteria* is busy at night when the candle-lit interior makes up for the romance that's absent during lunch with the clock-watching crowd. The food is good at anytime, though platters of aged cheese, mixed salami plates and home-made pastas are the attraction.

€€ **Joia**, Via Panfilo Castaldi 18, T02-2952 2124. Closed Sat and Sun lunch. A vegetarian restaurant with a Michelin star is no mean feat, but one in meat-loving Milan is quite extraordinary. Chef Pietro Leemann sees this as an opportunity rather than a drawback and his dishes dazzle with creativity, flavour and beautiful presentation.

€€ **L'Altra Pharmacia**, Via Rosmini 3, T02-345 1300. While it's a little off the tourist trail, this is an honest eatery serving up good sized portions of cooking that cures your ills. Ask for a recommendation from their interesting wine list to wash down their signature creamy risotto served in a round of Parmesan – just what the doctor ordered.

€€ **Nabucco**, Via Fiori Chiari 10, T02-860663. For years Nabucco has been the pick of via Fiori Chiari. A creative menu working on the popular premise of tradition with a twist, the light meat and fish dishes are outstanding. A notable wine list, elegant interior, and, during the warmer months, outdoor seating.

€€ Solferino 35, Via Solferino 35, T02-2900 5748. Closed Sat and Sun lunch. This cosy local restaurant is a firm favourite, with an excellent short menu and well-matched wine list. A tasty starter selection followed by anything cooked in the wood-fired oven (ask for the specials) is the way to graze the menu.

Cafés

Cova, Via Montenapoleone 8, T02-7600 5599. This restored tearoom is a classic destination on a shopping excursion, either for an espresso hit to help maintain the shopping pace or for a glass of prosecco to celebrate scoring a bargain designer get-up.

Viel, Via Manzoni 3e, corso Buenos Aires 15, T02-2951 6123. One of Milan's best-known producers of *frullati di frutta* (fruit shakes) and ice cream sorbets, Viel have been making their huge range of flavours since the 1940s.

West Milan *p30*

€€ Boccondivino, Via Giosué Carducci 17, T02-866 040. Closed Sun. If you're wondering why Italy is so revered for its cheeses, wines, hams and salamis, Boccondivino answers the question. Popular with locals who pick their way through plates of wonderful produce and select hard-to-source wines from the wine list.

Cafés

Caffè Litta, Corso Magenta 25, T02-805 7596. This lovely old café is an institution in Milan, as much for its art nouveau interior as its excellent coffee and snacks. The outdoor seating is just as popular for the corso Magenta people-watching.

Marchesi, Via S M alla Porta 11a, T02-876730. Don't let the endearingly old-fashioned window display and original interior here distract you from the excellent coffee and snacks – popular since 1824!

East Milan *p39*

€€ Da Giacomo, Via Sottocorno 6, T02-7602 3313. Closed Mon and Tue lunch. While this inconspicuous trattoria is ever-popular with Milan's business elite and fashion's heavy hitters, it's all about excellent seafood in convivial surroundings. The *gnocchetti* with prawns alone makes the trip to this unassuming neighbourhood worth the effort.

€€ Da Giannino L'Angolo d'Abruzzo, Via Rosolino Pilo 20, T02-2940 6526. Closed Mon. Unapologetically old-fashioned, this family-run trattoria serves up dishes from the Abruzzo region of central Italy. While some of the customers look older than time itself, the cooking is timeless.

South Milan *p41*

€€ Cantina Della Vetra, Papa Pio IV, T02-8940 3843. Closed Sat lunch. This rustic food and wine bar has a strong local following for the delights of the frequently changing blackboard menu. Excellent mixed plates of salami and accompanying *gnocco fritto* (puffy fried dough), as well as great wines, make this a good stop on the Navigli.

€€ El Brellin, Vicolo Dei Lavandai and Alzaia Naviglio Grande 14, T02-5810 1351. One of the heavyweight restaurants along the Navigli, this ristorante and popular aperitivo bar, situated in an old mill, is perfect for pre-dinner drinks followed by classic Milanese dishes. The outdoor garden is great for lunch.

€€ Officina 12, Alzaia Naviglio Grande 12, T02-8942 2261. Closed Mon and Sat-Tue lunch. There is nothing modest about this massively popular Navigli eatery: from the size of the local groups that come here, to the size of the tasty pizzas, to the size of the restaurant itself. While it's more romantic sitting alfresco, inside the atmosphere is contagious.

€ Fabbrica, Via Alzaia Naviglio Grande 70, T02-835 8297. The attraction is pretty straightforward at this popular pizza place – wonderful, simple wood-fired pizzas constantly heading out to 2 floors of hungry locals. It's open late, too, making it a solid

The Navigli

Aperitivo is first and foremost a Milanese ritual – don't let anyone tell you differently. So your night out sampling aperitivo spots – essentially a bar hop! – should begin with a stroll from the centre of Milan, starting from the **Duomo**, in the lovely late afternoon. This way you can do as the Milanese do and follow the locals who saunter here after work, taking it especially slowly during summer.

To get to the Navigli from the Duomo, follow shopping street **via Torino** until you come to a fork in the road: take the left prong, **corso di Porta Ticinese**. You'll soon come across the 16 striking columns of **San Lorenzo Maggiore** on your left. If it's a Friday or Saturday night, the piazza in front of the church, a popular meeting place, will be crowded with people sipping beers and sitting at the base of the columns chatting to their friends.

Walk under the arch where – if you're ready to start – you can imbibe at a local favourite, **Luca's Bar**. Continuing further down the street you'll no doubt see the neoclassical columns of **Porta Ticinese**. Continue on, then head right along piazza 24 Maggio. You'll now come across three bodies of water, the Darsena on your right, the **Naviglio Grande** directly ahead and the Naviglio Pavese to your left. Walk towards the Naviglio Grande where you'll see that there are streets running down each side of the waterway, the one on the left being Ripa di Porta Ticinese and the one on the right Alzalia Naviglio Grande. You can grab a quick drink at the outdoor bars that spill onto the bridge or head down **Alzalia Naviglio Grande** where some of Milan's best aperitivo bars are.

Your first aperitivo stop is **El Brellin** (see page 49), one of the local favourites for its much-coveted seating overlooking the water. Next you'll pass **Officina 12** (see page 49) where they do great pizzas (and even better steaks) – the

choice after a few aperitivo rounds along the Navigli.

€ Gnocco Fritto, Via Pasquale Paoli 2, T02-5810 0216. Just off the Navigli, this is the place where groups of locals go to line their stomachs before a night out, or head after they've realised that aperitivo snacks only go so far. The big attraction is huge plates of fresh *gnocco fritto* (puffy fried dough) which shares equal billing with delicious plates of cheese and cold cuts.

€ Le Vigne, Ripa di Porta Ticinese 61, T02-837 5617. Closed Sun. This honest little *osteria* is an endearing one, with a *piccolo* menu and a wine list that's a real page-turner for the grape buffs. Fantastic fresh pastas and great seasonal specials.

€ Luca & Andrea, Alzaia Naviglio Grande 34, T02-5810 1142. A long-time favourite on the Navigli, the languid nature of this enoteca belies the quality of the wines and the outstanding plates of cheese and *salumi misti* (mixed salami and ham).

€ Pizzeria Naturale, Via Edmondo de Amicis 24, T02-839 5710. The fantastic wood-fired oven front and centre gives diners a big hint as to what the specialty is here, but it's the wholemeal and gluten-free options that set this pizza place apart. Only a few tables, so get in early for some of the best pizza in town.

€ Pizzeria Tradizionale, Ripa di Porta Ticinese 7, T02-839 5133. One of the key eateries on the Navigli, **Pizzeria Tradizionale** does a roaring trade, with its outside tables packed with locals and visitors half an hour after opening every night. The big, puffy pizzas make their way to just about every table, but the locals also swear by the *fritto misto* (fried seafood).

atmosphere is lively, making it popular with groups. Next up is a local institution, **Luca & Andrea** (see page 50), where they serve delicious plates of cheese and meats as well as great wines. By now the place will be buzzing with locals perched on stools by the water or spilling across the pavement, so you can settle in and do some people-watching.

Next, if you're ready to have something serious to eat, you can keep heading down Alzaia Naviglio Grande to **Fabbrica** (see page 49), where the pizzas are some of Milan's best, or you can head over to the other side of the canal, crossing the footbridge at via Casale. On the other side of the canal there are a couple of casual eateries that are worth a look, including **Le Vigne** (see page 50), a friendly rustic *osteria* and **Gnocco Fritto** (see page 50), a buzzy place where you can soak up the liquor with some simple filling fare. Alternatively, you can head up Ripa di

Porta Ticinese. There are a few more bars you can stop at en route and if you still haven't found something that tempts your tastebuds, **Pizzeria Tradizionale** (see page 50) has plenty of atmosphere and outdoor cobblestone seating.

By now you might have seen crowds gathering a few doors up at **Rinomata Gelateria** (see page 51). Make a beeline here when you're ready for dessert. If you're not in the mood for gelato, you can check out the trinkets being sold outside by the stallholders at the head of Naviglio Pavese. Or, if you want to kick on, head down Naviglio Pavese and do a lap of the outdoor bars with their pumping soundtracks, which will provide you with plenty of options well into the night. You can also head back along corso di Porta Ticinese where wandering beside the canal, sipping a beer (bought from one of the late-night shops), is a local tradition – as is a toast to a good night out.

Cafés

Rinomata Gelateria, corner of Ripa di Porta Ticinese and viale Gloriziα, T02-5811 3877. One of the defining moments of summer in Milan is taking the edge off the sweltering heat at this venerable gelateria. Delightfully old-fashioned with fantastic flavours.

Bars and clubs

Apart from aperitivo of course – which begins after work or before dinner – the Milanese hit the bars late (after 2200) and hit the clubs even later (rarely before midnight). While bars are free, and there'll often be free snacks for drinkers, clubs often charge an admission fee (from around €10-20) however, this usually includes a drink. Some clubs have free nights, while others offer annual membership (check online) which is sometimes little

more than the cost of an entry fee yet guarantees you free entry and other perks. Many venues are closed during Aug.

Bars

Bar Brera, Via Brera 23, T02-877091. Daily 0700-0300. A Milan institution, it's hard to beat a sunny afternoon here people-watching on the cobblestone streets.
Bar Magenta, Via Carducci 13, T02-805 3808. Daily 0800-0300. The antidote for those who say Milan is reserved, this traditional remedy is best taken between 1700 and 2100, when aperitivo heats up.
Beige, Largo La Foppa 5, T02-659 9487. Mon-Sat 1200-0200. A relaxing bar and *enoteca*, it's reliable for a glass of good wine and excellent finger food for aperitivo.
Bhangra Bar, Piazza Sempione 1, T02-3493 4469, www.bhangrabar.it. Wed-Sun. Probably Milan's only Indian-inspired

aperitivo spread. Low-key hipsters frequent this bar, which turns more club-like as the night wears on.

Le Biciclette, Via Torti 1, T02-5810 4325, www.lebiciclette.eu. Mon-Sat 1800-0200, Sun 1230-0200. This former bicycle workshop pedals some of the best of aperitivo atmosphere in Milan – get there early.

Boccascena Café, Teatro Litta, corso Magenta 24, T02-805 5882. Daily 1000 till curtain close. Set in an 18th-century *palazzo*, this groovy bar belies all that's stuffy about theatre. Go for pre- or post-play drinks.

Diana Bar, Sheraton Diana Majestic Hotel, viale Piave 42, T02-20581, www.sheraton.com. Daily 1000-0200. The grande dame of aperitivo just keeps marching along with a stylish crowd, excellent cocktails and the choice of garden or groovy interior settings.

Huggy Bear, Piazza Sempione 3, T02-345 1614. 70s mood, great cocktails, plenty of retro music, and a cuddly vibe, of course.

Living, Piazza Sempione 2, T02-3310 0824, www.livingmilano.com. This former post office can have lines as long as its former incarnation did for the excellent aperitivo snacks. Arrive about 1700.

Luca's Bar, Colonne di S Lorenzo, corso di Porta Ticinese, T02-5810 0409. Far from the world of shiny hip bars full of designer furniture, low-key Luca's bar is all about the liquor. Go late.

Yguana, Via Papa Gregorio XIV 6, T02-8940 4195. Jungle-boogie vibe with wicker chairs, wicked cocktails and wonderful snacks.

Clubs

Café L'Atlantique, Viale Umbria 42, T02-202322, www.cafeatlantique.it. Tue, Wed, Fri and Sat 2100-0400, Thu and Sun 1930-0400, closed Jul and Aug. An upmarket club for the well heeled and well dressed, with quality DJs and drinks.

Gasoline Club, Via Bonnet 11a, T02-339 774 5797, www.discogasoline.it. Thu-Sun 2230-0400, closed Aug. This small club has fabulous gay nights.

Hollywood, Corso Como 15, T02-659 8996, www.discotecahollywood.com. Tue-Sun 2230-0400, closed Jul and Aug. Somewhat dated, this legendary club still manages to attract the rich and fatuous, from footballers to fashionistas. Dress accordingly.

Il Gattopardo Café, Via Piero della Francesca 47, T02-3453 7699, www.ilgattopardocafe.com. Tue-Sun 1800-0400. Located in a deconsecrated church, this club has plenty of baroque charm.

La Banque, Via B Porrone 6, T02-8699 6565, www.labanque.it. Tue-Thu 1800-0200, Fri-Sat 1800-0400, Sun 1900-0000, closed Aug. This former bank is a quite formal, club-style restaurant, bar and dance venue.

Magazzini Generali, Via Pietrasanta 16, T02-539 3948, www.magazzinigenerali. it. Wed-Sun 2200-0400, closed Jul and Aug. This converted warehouse is a happy home to everything from concerts to club nights. *JetLag* on Fri is a mixed-crowd marvel.

Old Fashion Café, Viale Emillio Alemagna 6, T02-805 6231, www.oldfashion.it. Daily 2300-0400. Labelling itself 'restaurant and rhythmic bar' is truth in advertising – great DJs, great drinks, and good vibe, even on weeknights.

Plastic, Viale Umbria 120, T02-733996. Thu-Sun 2200-0400, closed Aug. Once past the fire breathing door dragons (arrive early or fabulously late), you'll find durable **Plastic** one of the best mixed-crowd clubs in Italy.

Gay and lesbian

Gay and lesbian Milan has a notoriously fickle bar and club scene. Many bars and clubs are straight 6 nights of the week and have 1 great gay-friendly night a week, but the nights and the clubs change. The best thing to do is to contact Arcigay di Milano (www.arcigaymilano.org) which has membership cards to most gay venues. Despite the changeable nature, **Afterline** is a good choice for men, while **Sottomarino Giallo** is a dependable choice for women.

Afterline, Via Sammartini 25, T02-3651 9232, www.afterline.eu. Mon-Sat 2100-0200, Sun 1800-0200. The granddaddy of gay venues, this club has the best theme nights on what is essentially Milan's 'gay street'.

Ricci, Piazza della Republica 27, T02-669 4269, www.ilricci.com. Tue-Sun 1800-0200, closed Aug. A café and cake shop by day, the setting of the sun sees this place turn into one of Milan's most popular gay venues in the city.

Sottomarino Giallo, Via Donatello 2, T02-3663 6204, www.sottomarinogiallo.it. Wed and Sun 2300-0300, Fri and Sat 2300-0400, closed Aug. 'Yellow Submarine' remains the premier hangout for lesbian women of all ages who mingle over 2 floors with a bar and disco. Weekends are strictly gay.

🎭 Entertainment

Cinema
Anteospazio Cinema, Via Milazzo 9, T02-659 7732, www.spaziocinema.info. This art house film centre has 3 screens, a bookshop and café.

Arcobaleno Film Centre, Viale Tunisia 11, T02-2940 6054, www.cinenauta.it. Plays the latest releases – but bear in mind Italian cinemas have a tendency to dub rather than use subtitles.

Cineteca Italiana, Viale Vittorio Veneto 2, T02-7740 6300, www.cinetecamilano.it. This stronghold of Italian cinema has classics in the library – projected in their original language.

Music
Alcatraz, Via Valtellina 25, T02-6901 6352, www.alcatrazmilano.it. Fri-Sat 2200-0400. Club closed Jul and Aug. A venue that hosts big international acts such as Kanye West during the week, it's generally a dance club on weekends.

Blue Note, Via Borsieri 37, T02-6901 6888, www.bluenotemilano.com. Performances Mon-Sat 2100 and 2330, Sun 1800 and 2100. This Italian branch of the **Blue Note** franchise is an excellent one, with real atmosphere and great local and international acts.

Blues House, Via S Uguzzone 26, Villa San Giovanni, T02-3956 0756, www.blueshouse. it. Wed-Mon 2245-late. Way off the radar of inner-city Milan, this blues club is worth the trek if you know the players on the bill – not so much for the 'tribute' bands.

Forum, Via di Vittorio, Agasso, T02-488571, www.forumnet.it. A big, soulless, and acoustically challenged venue for major acts such as Bob Dylan.

Scimmie, Via Cardinale Ascanio Sforza 49, T02-8940 2874, www.scimmie.it. Daily 2000-0300. An atmospheric bar on the Navigli, Scimmie specializes in live music – especially jazz.

Theatre, opera and ballet
Auditorium di Milano, Largo Gustav Mahler, corso San Gottardo 42a, T02-4803 4803, www.auditoriumdimilano. org. Box office open Thu-Sun 1000-1900. This delightful former cinema is home to the Giuseppe Verde Symphonic Orchestra and hosts others.

Le Voci della Città, located at various historic churches around Milan, T02-3910 4149, www.levocidellacitta.it. 'The Voices of the City' concert programme includes orchestras, vocal ensembles, organ, choral and chamber music concerts, which take place in Milan's splendid churches, such as the Basilica di Sant'Ambrogio throughout the year. There's information online or available at the tourist office.

Piccolo Teatro di Milano: Teatro Strehler & Teatro Grassi, Via Rovello 2, T02-4241 1889, www.piccoloteatro.org. Box office open Mon-Sat 1000-1845. These 2 highly regarded theatres host quality productions as well as ballet.

Serate Al Museo, T02-8846 4526, www.comune.milano.it/dseserver/ labellaestate/. These summer 'Night at the Museum' events are held across the city and feature concerts and workshops. See the tourist office for programmes.

Teatro alla Scala, Via Filodrammatici 2, T02-7200 3744, www.teatroallascala.org.

This sumptuous 18th-century opera house has been restored to its former glory after a restoration and controversial additions (see page 26). Off-stage dramas have matched the onstage melodrama, but when the curtain goes up each year on 7 Dec for the start of the season that now runs most of the year – thanks to the renovations – all is forgiven. With the expanded backstage areas of the theatre, the sets can be works of art themselves – just like the performances of operas by Verdi, who had a wonderful creative career based in this very opera house. Sub-title screens built into the backs of the seats have also improved the experience of those coming to the opera for the first time. When you're in Milan, the best place to get tickets is the ticket office at **Galleria del Sagrato**, Piazza del Duomo, in the metro underpass (1200-1800). You can also purchase online from their website.
Teatro dal Verme, Via San Giovanni sul Muro 2, T02-8790 5201, www.dalverme.org. Box office open Tue-Sun 1100-2100. This delightful venue, built in the 1870s, has had several lives, but today it's home to theatrical events, concerts and operas.
Teatro Manzoni, Via Alessandro Manzoni 42, T02-763 6901, www.teatromanzoni. it. Box office open Mon-Sat 1000-1900, Sun 1100-1700. A favourite for its light comedies, musicals and Sun morning performances.

O Shopping

Opening hours vary remarkably from the enormous emporiums on corso Vittorio Emanuele II, which never seem to close, to the smaller stores which generally do business Mon-Sat 0930 or 1000, close for lunch at 1200 or 1300, then reopen 1600-1900. Those staying open on Sun close one weekday (usually Mon) and open late another afternoon (often Tue).

Art and antiques
The cobblestone streets of Brera, northeast of the Duomo, on via Brera and Solferino

in particular, are crammed with fine art galleries and antique shops, while those lining the Naviglio Grande tend to specialize in bric-a-brac and emerging artists. For more antique shops try the area around Sant'Ambrogio, on San Maurilio and via San Giovani. Milan also hosts a number of regular antique markets. If you're serious about buying local art, look out for the booklets 'Start Milano: Guida All'Arte Contemporanea' (start-mi.net).

Books
Panton's English Bookshop, Via Mascheroni 12, Angolo via Ariosto, T02-469 4468, www.englishbookshop.it. Author Peter Panton opened this cluttered English bookstore (Milan's first) in 1979. Specializes in rare and second-hand books.
Ricordi Media Stores, Galleria Vittorio Emanuele II, T02-8646 0272, www. lafeltrinelli.it. If Messaggerie Musicali doesn't have what you're looking for, find it here.

Clothing and accessories
You'll find fabulous fashion, shoes, accessories and jewellery on corso Vittorio Emanuele II. For exclusive designer wear, your first stop should naturally be the chic fashion quarter, the **Quadrilatero d'Oro** (see page 37). For more interesting fashion and jewellery, hit the hip boutiques on via Torino, corso di Porta Ticinese, and in and around Naviglio Grande.
10 Corso Como, Corso Como 10, T02-2900 2674, www.10corsocomo.com. When Italian Vogue editor Carla Sozzani opened this groundbreaking store in 1991 she started an inspired retail trend. This multi-brand fashion boutique, art gallery, gift store, book and music shop, restaurant, café and bar remains as stylish as ever.
Borsalino, Galleria Vittorio Emanuele 92, T02-8901 5436, www.borsalino.com. One of the country's oldest hat-makers, Giuseppe Borsalino started making beautifully crafted men's and women's hats in 1857. They're renowned for their fedoras.

Cavalli e Nastri, Via Brera 2, T02-7200 0449, www.cavallienastri.com. Fashion discoveries are a real delight here, one of Milan's first and still one of its best vintage clothing stores.

Colomba Leddi, Via Revere 3, T02-4801 4146, www.colombaleddi.it. Colomba Leddi has been creating stunning bespoke clothes for over a decade from her gorgeous atelier. Select your own fabrics and design or seek advice from a professional stylist.

Purple, Corso di Porta Ticinese 22, T02-8942 4476. The racks bulge with labels by sassy local designers, much of them stitched together from recycled fabrics, some created exclusively for Purple.

Sermoneta, Via della Spiga 46, T02-7631 8303, www.sermonetagloves.com. An Italian institution, **Sermoneta** has been producing the finest quality Italian leather and suede gloves since 1965. The driving gloves are a must on a Lakes road trip. There's a mind-boggling array of colours and styles and staff ensure your gloves are properly fitted.

Cosmetics and perfume

Acqua di Parma, Via Gesù 3, T02-7602 3307, www.acquadiparma.it. Created in the 1930s, and originally made for men, this one-of-a-kind fragrance now has a female counterpart, Profumo, and a line of sensual body products.

Calé Fragranze d'Autore, Via S Maria Alla Porta 5, T02-8050 9449, www.cale.it. Let the aromas of rare European perfumes waft over you at this elegant store – then take some home!

La Speziale, Corso Buenos Aires 59, T02-2940 0644, www.laspeziale.it. Can't find that special scent? Then have a personalized fragrance made just for you – or your own essential oils prepared.

Department stores

With so many fabulous and fascinating shops in Milan, it's hard to imagine why you'd want a department store other than during the end-of-season sales when they're known for their bargains. Try swish La Rinascente

(piazza del Duomo, T02-875653, Mon-Sat 0900-2200 and Sun 1000-2000) or the more affordable **COIN** (piazza Cinque Giornate, T02-5519 2083, Mon-Sat 0900-2000).

Design products

Design junkies should make a beeline for the cutting-edge contemporary design stores on corsos Venezia, Monforte and Europa.

Alessi, Corso Matteotti 9, T02-795726, www.alessi.com. Pick up a quirky souvenir from the flagship store of the makers of the Magic Bunny toothpick holder and iconic products such as their Starck-designed 3-legged juicer.

Da Driade, Via Manzoni 30, T02-7602 0398, www.driade.com. This frescoed neoclassical mansion is home to Antonia and Enrico Astori's contemporary design solutions, as well as chic furniture and lighting products from international designers who share their style philosophy.

Kartell, Via Turati and Carlo Porta 1, T02-659 7916, www.kartell.it. Milan's plastic pioneer, Kartell is synonymous with clever designs, from Ron Arad's Bookworm shelf (1994) to the Louis Ghost chair (2002) and Optic cubes (2006).

Momo Design, Galleria San Babila 4/A, T02-7601 6168, www.momodesign.com. Sleek motorcycle helmets, sunglasses, leatherwear, watches and other cool accessories to go with that Vespa you're planning on taking home.

SAG '80, Via Giovanni Boccaccio 4, T02-481 5380, www.sag80.com. Covet contemporary design products by the biggest names – Artemide, B&B Italia, Boffi, Cappellini, Dada, Driade, Flos, Knoll, Matteograssi, Minotti, Vitra and Zanotta – at this 1-stop design shop.

Food and drink

Enoteca Cotti, Via Solferino 42, T02-6572 995, www.enotecacotti.it. The Cotti brothers have run these atmospheric cellars since 1952, supplying wine buffs with fine Italian offerings – a great source for collection-quality vintages, especially those of Lombard growers.

Giovanni Galli, Victor Hugo 2, T02-8646 4833, www.giovannigalli.com. Specializing in 'maronni, canditi, fondenti' (chestnuts, candies, fondants). There are also delectable chocolates, pralines, marzipan, amaretti, and tinned pastels.

Peck, Via Spadari 9, T02-802 3161, www.peck.it. Established in 1883, elegant **Peck** boasts 3 floors of gastronomic goodies, making it a perfect for picnics or gourmet gift-shopping. Ground floor counters and shelves are crammed with aged proscuitto, Parma ham, truffles, olive oil, pastries, gelato and freshly prepared meals for the picnic basket. Upstairs there's a café, chocolates, sweets, teas and fresh coffee beans, while downstairs is a wine cellar and champagne bar.

Jewellery

Mon Bijou, Via Pontaccio 2, T02-8058 3197. Milanese jewellery designer Alessandra Moro creates feminine jewellery from semi-precious gems that is charmingly retro in style.

Pellini, Corso Magenta 11, T02-7201 0569, www.pellini.it. With its antique furniture, this delightful shop is the perfect setting for owner Donatella Pellini's unique pieces.

Kidswear and toys

Città del Sole, Via Orefici 13, T02-8646 1683, www.cittadelsole.it. Need to keep the kids busy in the back seat on those long drives? This fantastic toy shop stocks a huge range of good old-fashioned toys including frisbees, board games, jigsaw puzzles, model kits, activity books, and hand puppets.

I Pinco Pallino, Via della Spiga 42, T02-781931, www.ipincopallino.it. This children's clothes store, complete with crystal chandelier and kiddie fashion TV, specializes in the most fashionable Italian kids' wear around.

Markets

Mercato Comunale, Darsena, piazza XXIV Maggio. Mon-Sat. Covered market for fresh fruit and veg on the Darsena.

Ripa di Porta Ticinese, Naviglio Grande. Last Sun of month). Huge art, antiques and bric-a-brac market lines the canal.

Strada Alzaia, Naviglio Grande. Sat all day. Lively flea market relocated from Viale Gabriele d'Annunzio and crammed with unusual stuff.

Via Fiori Chiari, Brera. 3rd Sat of month. High quality antique market specializing in fine antiques and art.

Viale Papiniano, Tue and Sat mornings. Fresh local produce (perfect for picnic supplies) and cheap clothes.

Novelty

Luisa Cevese Riedizioni, Via San Maurilio 3, T02-801088, www.riedizioni.com. This Milanese designer creates innovative recycled plastic and textile products, from handbags and raincoats to notebooks and cushions, all delightfully embedded with vibrant scraps of fabric, yarn and threads – it's all industrial waste!

Moroni Gomma, Corso Matteotti 14, T02-796220, www.moronigomma.it. Fun stuff for home and leisure-time that makes fabulous gifts and souvenirs, from retro-looking Tivoli radios to Mini Gioco Football games.

Stationery

Fabriano, Via Ponte Vetero 17, T02-7631 8754, www.fabrianoboutique.com. Handmade paper manufacturers since 1872, **Fabriano** also stocks fine quality, handmade, Italian leather-bound photo albums, diaries, notepads, business-card holders and wallets.

Papier, Via San Maurilio 4, off Via Torino, T02-865221, www.papier-milano.it. Beautiful handmade textured writing and wrapping paper embedded with flower petals, leaves and the like, along with exquisite pens, desk-sets, and photo frames with gems and beads.

⚙ What to do

Football

San Siro Stadium, Via Piccolomini 5, T02-4870 0457. Milan's 2 major league football clubs, **AC Milan** (acmilan.com) and **FC Internazionale Milano** (generally known as 'Inter' or 'Inter Milan', inter.it) play at this famous stadium, which is hardly ever called its real name – **Stadio Giuseppe Meazza**. Football fans will enjoy the museum and tour (T02-404 2432, www.sansiro.net, open daily 1000-1700, €13 adults, €10 under 14) dedicated to the stadium and the 2 teams that built their reputation here. Tickets to matches are available from branches of Banca Popolare di Milano or from the websites of the 2 teams.

Language

Dante Alighieri, Piazza le Cadorna 9, T02-7201 1294, www.dantealighieri.org. This long-established school offers an extensive range of Italian courses suitable for beginners or for those wishing to study at an Italian-speaking university.

Motoring

Autodromo Nazionale Monza, Via Vedano 5, Parco di Monza, T039-24821, www.monzanet.it. This legendary car racing track, generally known just as 'Monza', is only a short drive away from Milan and is the host of a round of the Formula One Grand Prix circus. The race is seen as the 'home' grand prix of Ferrari. If you're not there for this red flag waving Ferrari love-fest in Sep, you can actually take a lap of the famous circuit in your street vehicle for just €40. Specific dates are available from the website.

Sightseeing

Autostradale, departure point at via Marconi, nr Duomo, T02-3391 0794, www.autostradale.it. The **Autostradale** bus company runs a 3-hr bus tour of the city (except Mon). Perfect if you want to knock over the key sights of the city quickly before going shopping guilt-free. One of the best aspects of the tour is the guaranteed visit to da Vinci's *The Last Supper* – it can be hard to get tickets at short notice otherwise. MaTM (T02-4803 6999, matmbus.com) offer a tour with a similar itinerary.

Centro Guide, T02-8645 0433, www.centroguidemilano.net. **Centro Guide** provides official guides who are proficient in English (and a number of other languages) and are experts in their chosen field. The cost of €100 for 3 hrs covers up to 25 people.

Ciao Milano Tourist Tram, Departure point at piazza Castello, T02-7252 4301. Several restored 1920s-era trams run from Apr-Oct, going past the main points of interest, with headphones and multilingual commentary.

Navigli Cruises, Via Copernico 42, T02-667 9131, www.naviglilombardi.it. Running in the warmer months on weekends, these tours glide down the Navigli waterways, which were originally designed by da Vinci in the 1400s to transport goods and were still active until the Second World War.

Sightseeing Milano, Foro Bonaparte 76, T02-867131, www.milano.city-sightseeing.it. This 'Hop-On Hop-Off' bus has 2 lines around the city with tickets valid for 24 hrs (€20 adults, €10 ages 5-15) and commentary in several languages. Some sections of the trips do overlap, so it's best to check the routes to decide which satisfies your interests.

Zani Viaggi, Foro Bonaparte 76, T02-867131, www.zaniviaggi.it. This well-established travel agency is a one-stop-shop for a wide range of trips, including Milan shopping expeditions and aperitivo tours. This excellent travel agency also organizes tours to other parts of Lombardy including all the lakes, Como, Bergamo and Verona, as well as visits further afield.

ⓘ Directory

Medical services Hospital Ospedale Maggiore, 'Policlinico', via F Sforza 35, T02-55031. **Pharmacy**, Carlo Erba, piazza Duomo, T02-8646 4832.

Contents

The Lakes

Lake Como

Lake Como is the shining star of the lakes. When people dream of the Italian Lakes, you bet it's Lago di Como that they're envisioning. Its undeniable beauty, as well as its strategic location as a link between Italy, central Europe and beyond, has made it a coveted address through the ages with artists, artisans and, more recently, American actor George Clooney, all of whom have made the villas skirting these turquoise waters a base for inspiration and reflection.

Shaped like an upside down 'Y', Como sits at the lower tip of the western arm and is the most pragmatic of locations on the lake. The pedestrianized area of the *centro storico* is punctuated by the splendid Duomo; however, it's the attractive waterfront that everyone's attention always returns to.

As you explore the lake further, snaking around the foreshore and hugging the mountains that surround the lake, small towns, villas and sublime vistas appear regularly. Delightful Bellagio has an enviable position and good shopping on its steep cobbled streets, while Tremezzo has the lovely extensive gardens and handsome structures of Villa Carlotta nearby. There is plenty to explore on Lake Como and while summer is the best weather for enjoying the lakes, the shoulder seasons either side of summer are far less frenetic—after all, you're coming here to relax, aren't you?

Como → *For listings, see pages 73-77. See map, page 64.*

Cradled at the base of a mountain and sprawled around a pretty curve of the lake, the town of Como not only has a stunning setting, but it's also one of the lakes' most characterful towns, with atmospheric cobblestone lanes and lively little piazzas where locals like to socialize over coffee or aperitivi. Como also has the added appeal of being one of the lake's few year-round destinations; it is as enjoyable in winter, when there's mist over the lake and the streets are lit with Christmas lights, as it is in the summer, when the place to be is by the water with the locals on a balmy evening.

Arriving in Como
Getting there Trains arrive at the main station **Como San Giovanni** or **Como Lago** ① *www.lenord.it*, on the lake. The bus station is **SPT Linea** ① *via Asiago 16/18, T031-247111.*

Tourist information ① *Piazza Cavour, T031-269712, www.lakecomo.org, Mon-Sat 0900-1300 and 1430-1800, Sun (in summer only) 0930-1230.*

Old town and Duomo
Many visitors make the town of Como their base for exploring the lake, which they do by water, hopping on and off boats over the course of a few days. Other travellers stay a couple of nights in Como's old town, then drive around the perimeter of the lake spending a night or two in each of, say, Cernobbio, Tremezzo or Menaggio on the western shore, Bellagio at the lake's centre, and then perhaps Varenna, on the eastern shore, before returning to Como. Arrive by car, however, and you'll probably push on, the city appearing rather unattractive with industry all around; arrive by train at the edge of the old town with the water opposite, and you won't want to leave.

Once ensconced in Como's *centro storico* you'll soon realise this is one elegant little city. While Como's foreshore is dotted with imposing architectural monuments, lovely waterside parks, and busy bars and gelaterias, the labyrinthine old centre is blessed with lively piazzas, stylish boutiques and atmospheric restaurants – making it very hard to drag oneself away to explore the rest of the lake. While the cobblestone pedestrian-only lanes of Como's compact old town are enjoyable enough to wander, unlike other lakeside towns, Como actually has a handful of sights worth seeing, including some splendid churches and fine museums. Add to that, during the warmer months, Como's piazzas and gardens host jazz, classical music and world music concerts. Opposite the lake and marina, and at the centre of the old town's waterfront, **piazza Cavour** is an elegant square lined with alfresco cafés on one side and the tourist office on the other. From here, the atmospheric streets of Como's old town or Cortesella radiate; the city's history is on show everywhere, from its Roman beginnings evident in the grid-like structure and ruins of **Porta Pretoria**, the Roman gate, to the remains of the medieval walls around the old town perimeter, to the Romanesque city gate of **Porta Torre** at piazza Vittoria.

Como's best churches include **Chiesa di San Fedele**, named after the saint who brought Christianity to Como, which is a this fine Romanesque church, built in 1120 and just a short stroll from the Duomo. It has a beautiful, intricately carved medieval door. Another fine church is the **Basilica di Sant' Abbondio**, which is another 11th-century Romanesque church with well preserved 13th-century Gothic frescoes; most of the intricate stonework was done by the famous Maestri Comaciniis at the Museo Civico. **Chiesa di Sant' Agostino**

Lakeside promenade

Splendidly set around the curve of Lake Como and nestled at the foot of densely wooded mountains, the city of Como has an enviable lakeside location that's best appreciated with an amble along the waterfront.

Start your saunter on the lake's southern side at gracious **Villa Olmo** ① *via Cantoni 1, T031-571979, if nothing's on, it should be open Mon-Fri 0930-1200 and 1500-1800, €7/3.50; gardens: summer 0800-2300 and winter 0700-1900, free.* This regal 18th-century neoclassical mansion boasts elegant, geometrical-patterned gardens, with manicured lawns at the front overlooking the lake, and a shady forest of parkland out back. Designed in 1780 by celebrated Swiss architect Simone Cantoni as a summer villa for the aristocratic Odescalchi family, it is now owned by Como municipality and used for exhibitions. It's not always possible to see the sumptuous interior, but it's just as enjoyable to wander round the wonderful gardens.

From here, stroll the lovely lakeside path, **Passeggiata di Villa Olmo**, through the elegant residential Borgovico suburb, passing **Chiesa di San Giorgio** and **Piazzale Somaini**, to via Puecher. Here you'll find three striking landmarks, the **Monumento ai Caduti** (Monument to the Fallen), **Tempio Voltiano** (Temple to Alessandro Volta), and **Monumento alla Resistenza** (Monument to the Resistance). Erected in 1930 as a memorial to Como's 650 fallen First World War heroes, the imposing 33-m high **Monumento ai Caduti** was designed by architect brothers Attilio and Giuseppe Terragni, based on 1914 sketches by futurist architect Antonio Sant'Elia. The white neoclassical **Tempio Voltiano** ① *viale Marconi, T031-574705, Apr-Sep Tue-Sun 1000-1200 and 1500-1800, Oct-Mar Tue-Sun 1000-1200 and 1400-1600, €3,*) is a commemorative monument and small museum dedicated to Alessandro Volta, Como's famous scientist. Follow the lakefront Lungolago Mafalda di Savoia to the adjoining leafy public gardens for the

is a 14th-century church with a beautiful baroque interior, decorated with frescoes, and an elegant cloister.

The main attraction of Como's *centro storico* is its monumental **Duomo** ① *Piazza del Duomo, T031-265244, daily 0900-1830, free.* Considered to be a great example of 14th-century transitional architecture, blending Gothic and Renaissance styles, architectural buffs will enjoy identifying elements from the different periods, such as the pretty Gothic rose window or the portal's two Renaissance statues of Como locals Pliny the Elder and Pliny the Younger (protected behind wire mesh). Once inside, there's a beautifully decorated rococo dome, an intricately carved 16th-century choir, and wonderful paintings and tapestries from the 16th and 17th centuries. Adjoining the Duomo is the striking striped pink, grey and white marble **Broletto**, the old town hall, built in 1215, but reduced in size in 1477 to accommodate the Duomo. The piazza del Duomo cafés provide a perfect spot from which to appreciate both – with a gelato of course!

The **Musei Civici Como** ① *Museo Archeologico and Museo Storico: Palazzo Giovio, piazza Medaglie d'Oro 1, T031-252550, Civiche Raccolte d'Arte and Palazzo Volpi: via Diaz 86, Tue-Sat 0930-1230 and 1400-1700, Sun 1000-1300, €3,* is actually four museums that fall under the umbrella of the Civic Museums of Como: the Museo Archeologico (Archaeological Museum), Museo Storico (Historical Museum), the Civiche Raccolte D'Arte (the Civic Art Gallery, also known simply as the Pinacoteca or Picture Gallery), and **Tempio Voltiano**

Monumento alla Resistenza. Inaugurated in 1983, this unusual memorial to victims of the Second World War consists of bronze sheets engraved with the names of the dead, with touching quotations from the victims.

Stroll out to the end of the *diga foranea* (breakwater), a narrow boardwalk opposite the park, for the best views of Como and the action on the water. From here you have a close-up view of the boats coming and going from the *imbarcadero* (jetty).

Continue along the tree-lined lakeside promenade beside Lungo Lario Trento to Lungo Lario Trieste at the end, perhaps the prettiest stretch of all. Seat yourself on a bench beneath the trees, with a view of the bustling lake action framed between the trunks, and you'll think to yourself this is quintessential Como. The promenade is especially lively on summer evenings when locals are out jogging, walking their dogs, canoodling, or, having lined up for ice cream at **Gelateria Ceccato** (see page 75) opposite, out strolling with gelato in hand.

If you're thirsty, grab a waterside table at the simple kiosk-bar **Al Molo** (see page 76), which boasts one of Como's best sunset viewing spots; otherwise, continue along Lungo Lario Trieste, making a note to return later. At piazza de Gasperi you'll see the **Funicolare per Brunate** (see below).

From here on, along viale Geno, you'll be strolling one of Como's most tranquil lakefront stretches, with lawn on your left that's ideal for sprawling out on with a picnic (it's a favourite dinner spot for local students sharing beers and take-away), while on your right you'll get a close peek at some of Como's most beautiful and affluent homes. It's hard to know which way to look.

At the end of the street, you'll come to **Villa Geno**, an elegant mansion used for weddings and functions, and from the point, gorgeous views across the lake to the seaplanes landing and taking off. By now it must be time for that aperitivo!

(the Temple to Alessandro Volta; see box, opposite). Spread over two palaces, the **Museo Archeologico** is crammed with fascinating artefacts, from Neolithic, Egyptian, Greek, and Roman times. Items of local relevance include decorative vessels from Como dating to the sixth century BC and artefacts from the Italians' battle for liberation from the Austrians that took place in the hills above Como. The **Museo Storico** has an interesting collection of textiles, ceramics and manuscripts, but most impressive are the exhibition of costumes, textiles and lace from the 17th and 19th centuries. The **Pinacoteca** plays host to some absorbing temporary shows but also houses engaging permanent exhibitions of painting, sculpture, graphic design and architectural models from the early medieval period through to the 20th century, including work by local artists. Most notable is the Romanesque collection formed from Como's various churches, abstract art from the Gruppo Como, and the architectural drawings by futurist architect Giuseppe Terragni including those for the Asilo Sant'Elia, a Como school.

Southern and western Como → *For listings, see pages 73-77.*

Como's western shore is quintessential Lake Como: from refined Cernobbio, at the southern end on the outskirts of Como, with Villa d'Este, the grande dame of hotels, to tiny villages with their stone houses and cobblestone alleys, to colossal villa-gardens that dot the shores all the way up to Tremezzo and Menaggio. Explore by car and you'll be eagerly looking for places to pull up at every turn in the road, so you can peer over fences and snap photos. Explore by boat and you'll be keen to get off at every ferry stop to do the same. Spend a few days (or more) here and you can do both!

Cernobbio

Only 5 km from Como, leafy Cernobbio is like a gracious suburb. Its two main attractions are the sumptuous **Villa d'Este** (see page 73), boasting sprawling gardens dotted with splendid fountains and marble statues that are open to the public and worth exploring, and Villa Erba.

Film director Luchino Visconti (see box, opposite) had fond memories of childhood summers spent at the beautiful **Villa Erba** ① *Largo Luchino Visconti 4, Cernobbio, T031-3491, www.villaerba.it*. His love for the lakeside ancestral home permeated some of his films, most evident in the ball scene in *The Leopard*. Visconti returned to the villa to rehabilitate

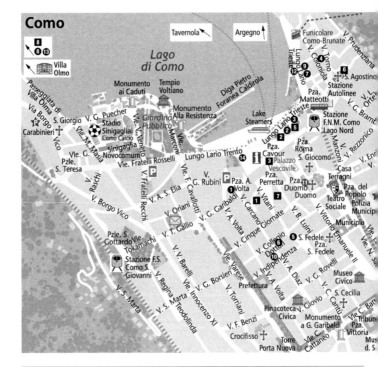

Luchino Visconti and Villa Erba

One of Como's favourite sons is renowned film director, Luchino Visconti (1906–1976). Considered the father of Italian Neo-realism, Visconti's films won acclaim for their realistic depiction of social problems in Italy during and after the Second World War. His film *Ossessione* (Obsession, 1942), based on the novel *The Postman Always Rings Twice*, was highly influential for its use of non-professional actors, natural camera movement and an 'authenticity'

created by hidden cameras. Born into an aristocratic dynasty, Visconti was able to use his connections and status to further his foray into directing – friendships with Coco Chanel and Maria Callas propelled his career. In later years, Visconti's films became more personal – films such as *Rocco and his Brothers* (1960), *The Leopard* (1963) and *Death in Venice* (1971) are seen as some of his greatest, all reflecting his memories of Lake Como in some way.

after becoming ill at the height of his career, but died four years later. Built by the family to entertain illustrious guests, the 19th-century mannerist villa was indeed lavish and in 2003 was restored to its former splendour. Now part of an exhibition and conference complex, the first floor Luchino Visconti rooms have been established as a museum dedicated to the director and the special bond he had with the villa. While the rooms are theoretically open to the public, they close when booked for conferences or special events. Visits are by appointment only, so Visconti fans (and anyone who loves snooping in beautiful houses) should book well in advance.

N

500 metres
500 yards

Where to stay
Albergo Del Duca 1
Albergo Terminus 2
Barchetta Excelsior 3
Palace Hotel 5
Quarcino 6
Tre Re 7
Villa Flori 8

Restaurants
Alessandro Volta 1
Bar Del Terme 2
Gelateria Ceccato 3
Il Carrettiere 4
Il Pinzimonio 5
Il Solito Posto 6
Il Vecchio Borgo 7
Joy 8
L'Antica Riva 9
Le Soste Ristorante 10
Nova Comum 11
Pizzeria La Darsena 12
Raimondi 13
Riva Café 14

Cernobbio to Tremezzo

After Cernobbio the narrow road snakes around the coast, which is dotted with palatial villas boasting palm-filled gardens, and delightful diminutive villages. **Colonno** has a labyrinthine old centre of stone arches over cobbled paths. **Sala Comacina** is home to the historic San Rocco chapel, a pretty little marina, and just offshore the overgrown **Isola Comacina**. Smattered with the ruins of old churches, it's Como's only island, and a bit of an artists' retreat. **Mezzegra** is where Mussolini and his mistress Claretta Petacci were killed in 1944. From the elegant village of **Lenno** you can walk about 20 minutes along the leafy peninsula to the splendid gardens at **Villa del Balbianello** (see box, page 66), which had a small part in the movie *Casino Royale* – where James Bond recuperated. And speaking of movies, a certain

Lake Como gardens

Lake Como is most famous for its splendid lakeside villas and their celebrated gardens. Spend any length of time here, especially in spring and summer, and the memories you'll come away with are of the ever-visible splashes of colour from azaleas, camellias, rhododendrons and bougainvillea, and of the fresh woody fragrances of cedar, cypress, juniper and pine. Boat around the lake and you'll be wishing you could hop off, climb over the garden walls, and sneak in for a look. Fortunately, there are a few gardens that are open to the public (so no wall-climbing necessary!), including Villa del Balbianello at Lenno, Villa Carlotta at Tremezzo, and Villa Monastero at Varenna (see page 71).

Villa del Balbianello ① *Via Comoedia, Lenno, T0344-56110, www.fondoambiente. it. Mar-Nov Tue and Thu-Sun 1000-1800; villa €7, garden €5, combined ticket €8/11 (with/without reservation). Imbarcadero: Lenno.* Stunningly located on the edge of Lenno, on a small, steep headland overlooking the lake, Villa del Balbianello was built in 1787 by Cardinal Angelo Maria Durini, but is more famous as the home of 20th-century explorer Count Guido Monzino who bequeathed

his beloved house to his country. Architecturally, aside from its graceful loggia, there's not a lot that's notable about the enormous lemon villa exterior. Rather, it's the alluring location and enchanting gardens that are special.

Inside the villa there's a fascinating collection of precious objects, art and antiques, including pre-Columbian, Chinese, and African art, and beautiful 18th-century French and English furniture. The Expedition Room contains personal mementoes, photos, flags, and memorabilia from Monzino's trips, including the eight-dog sledge he used to reach the North Pole in 1971. The Map Room in the loggia contains geographical charts Monzino used, along with antique prints of the lake. In the adjoining library are volumes of books Monzino amassed, comprising the research materials he used to plan trips. Today these represent one of the most complete collections of books on alpine and polar expeditions.

The luxuriant gardens are the highlight, however, with their multiple levels, sweeping staircases and panoramic terraces with unparalleled lake and Alpine vistas. Spilling down the steep hillside, with slopes of manicured lawn separated by neat hedges and foliage, the gardens

Hollywood star also has a rather grand villa in a certain village somewhere around here, but we'll let the man have his privacy.

Tremezzo
The stretch of coast around Tremezzo, known as the Tremezzina Riviera, is quintessential Lake Como, with its verdant hills, luxuriant gardens, belle époque villas and boats bobbing in the tranquil water offshore. Locals and regulars (those who return annually) claim that the air is more fragrant here and the lake is at its most serene. Tremezzo's main sight is elegant **Villa Carlotta** (see box, opposite) and its lovely botanic gardens.

Menaggio
Menaggio is probably one of Lake Como's more bustling villages, with a living, breathing authenticity that the other holiday spots don't have. There's decent

are unique in that they don't fit into either the ornate geometrical Italian form or the wild romantic English garden style that were fashionable at the time. They're an entrancing combination of the two, with shaded paths adorned with marble statues and potted shrubs on the one hand, and the wild wooded parkland on the other.

Villa Carlotta ① *Via Regina 2, Tremezzo, T0344-40405, www.villacarlotta.it. Apr-Sep 0900-1800, Mar and Oct 0900-1130 and 1400-1630, €7. Imbarcadero: Villa Carlotta or Cadenabbia.* Originally built in 1690 for a Milanese noble, the palatial pale pink Villa Carlotta was sold in 1801 to politician and patron of the arts, Battista Sommariva. It was Sommariva who started to develop the gardens and establish an exquisite art collection that drew travellers doing the Grand Tour (see box, page 98). However, it wasn't until the second half of the 19th century, when Princess Marianne of Nassau bought the mansion and gave it to her daughter Carlotta as a wedding gift, that the property was transformed into the thing of splendour it is today.

Carlotta's husband, George II of Saxen-Meiningen, was a passionate botanist and it was he and Carlotta who created the 14 acres of gardens that can be visited today. The front terraced Italian garden is the most dramatic (symmetrical staircases, geometrically arranged flowerbeds, hedges, fishponds, statues, fountains, and its famous 'tunnels' of citrus trees), but the sprawling botanical gardens that encircle the villa are even more impressive. Paths meander through the magnificent woods and gardens, and while there is a café and snack bar in the greenhouse, there are several lovely picnic spots, so bring your hamper.

Also worth an hour or two of your time is the restored neoclassical villa. The ground floor's museum has highlights including a high relief depicting the *Entrance of Alexander the Great in Babylon* commissioned by Napoleon for the Pantheon in Paris in the Marble Room (room 1), fine marble statues of saints from Milan's Duomo in the Cameos room (room 3), a splendid statue of Eros and Psyche, carved from one piece of Carrara marble, by Antonio Tadolini (room 7), the beautiful *Last Adieu of Romeo and Juliet* (1823) by Francesco Hayez (room 8), and an exquisite decorative ceiling (room 9). The first floor has rooms furnished in the original period style, giving a fantastic insight into how Italian aristocrats lived at the time.

shopping and a lively town square lined with restaurants and cafés, and a busy ferry dock, with good connections to all parts of the lake (many residents commute to work in Switzerland or Como). Parking is more plentiful than at most of the villages, making it easier to explore. There's a pretty lakeside promenade that runs the length of the town, boasting benches filled with romantic young Italians reading books and tourists texting home.

Bellagio

Bellagio is bewitching, but while it's decidedly touristy, it's undoubtedly Como's most romantic destination, boasting tranquil parks and meandering paths made for hand-holding, intimate waterfront restaurants and alfresco cafés more suited to couples than families or friends, and lakeside benches apparently installed for canoodling. Besides, apart from strolling the *lungolargo* (waterside promenade), touring the villa gardens,

Outdoor activities

Lago di Como offers visitors a wonderful array of ways to enjoy the crisp air, superb scenic vistas, and the languorous lake itself.

One of the first things you should do to get an overview of the area is to take the steep and slightly daunting **funicular** to the town of Brunate, some 720 m above the town of Como. If you're here on a clear day the views are phenomenal and strolling around the village of Brunate is also worth your time. If you're feeling in need of some exercise, you can walk back down to Como or head off into the hills on one of the many hikes that originate from here.

Given that Lake Como is often seen as a glamorous destination, taking a scenic seaplane flight from Como across the lakes is a popular option. Aero Club Como ① *viale Masia, 44, Como, T0315-74495, www.aeroclubcomo.com*, offers scenic flights that do a loop of the Como leg of the lake. On a clear day, the views are spectacular, especially if there is snow around on the mountains.

Staying on the water, there are plenty of ways to enjoy the lake. Catching the **ferry** ① *www.navigazionelaghi.it*, from Como to Bellagio (one of the must-see destinations on the lake) is an excellent way to see the villages and towns along the way from the water, which is where they look the prettiest. For only €10.40 it's a bargain, though check the timetables well ahead of time in the winter months to avoid disappointment.

Less of a bargain, but far more Clooney-esque is hiring a **speedboat** ① *www.comolakeboats.it, www.mostes-faggeto.com*, and charting your own watery path around the lake. Neither girls in bikinis nor macho James Bond-like men are included in the boat hire fee, which is around €60 per hour for a boat that carries five people.

There are several slower ways of seeing the lake. **Sailing** and **windsurfing** are best at the northern end of the lake due to the better and more consistent winds called the *breva*. Dervio, north of Bellano, is the best base for sailing, where there is a great sailing school, Orza Minore ① *www.orzaminore.com*. Windsurfers tend to congregate at Domaso (further north and on the west side of the lake), where the windsurfing centre ① *www.breva.ch*,

exploring the steep stairways of the *centro storico*, and dining in fine restaurants, there's actually very little to do in Bellagio.

Still, with its pretty pastel buildings spilling down the steep hillside, its quaint *centro storico* cradled by dense forest and parkland spiked with cypress trees, and its pretty lakeside promenade dotted with palms and flowerbeds, Bellagio offers what for many travellers is the quintessential Como experience.

While the drive from Como, along a hillside-hugging road (little more than one lane in places), is certainly dramatic, it can't beat arriving by water from the western shore. From the ferry, Bellagio is breathtaking, and it appears even more enchanting each moment it comes closer into view. Bellagio's stunning location in the most spectacular part of Lake Como is what makes it so special. On a headland at the tip of the Triangolo Lariano, the mountainous slither of land between Como and Lecco that splits the lake into two branches, it gives fantastic lake and Alpine views.

La Punta Spartivento After alighting from the ferry, day-trippers make a beeline for La Punta Spartivento ('the point that divides the wind'), the northernmost tip of the peninsula and most tranquil part of Bellagio. Here you'll find an attractive marina and is highly regarded, offering lessons for all ages and skill levels and they also have catamarans for hire. **Kayaking** (kayaks are also best hired from the windsurf centre) is also a popular way of enjoying the lake while allowing you to be a bit of a water-based snoop, seeing how the rich and nouveau riche decorate their little lakeside villas and gardens.

Back on land, it's important to note that **driving** around the lake can be more frightening than the **funicular** if you're not used to the narrow donkey tracks that sometimes double as roads around the lake.

Riding a **bike** (try Como Bike ① *via Grandi 15*, along the lake's waterfront is also a lovely way to spend an afternoon and all the tourist offices have brochures and maps detailing possible itineraries with distances and durations. **Mountain biking** ① *www.bellagio-mountains.it*, is increasingly popular, particularly around Bellagio. The same company that rents mountain bikes, The Caval Calario Club ① *www.bellagio-mountains.it*, also offers horse-riding – another popular activity around the lakes.

Once you've tackled some of these fun lake-focused activities, you need to try one of the most popular lakeside activities of all – a sunset drink! Wherever you are at the end of the day, toast yourself – you've more than likely earned it.

One of the most enjoyable things to do on Lake Como is simply to walk, through lush semi-tropical botanical gardens or along the waterside. Almost all of the lake's villages have cobblestone paths meandering through them, mule trails in the hills above the towns and footpaths that run by the water's edge. The **Greenway del Lago di Como** (www.greenwaydellago.it) is a specially created route connecting these paths all the way from Colonno to Cadenabbia di Griante, allowing you to enjoy a wonderful, uninterrupted 10.5 km walk along the lake, passing palatial villas, sprawling gardens, Roman ruins, and spectacular views en route. The itinerary is set out in a handy little booklet with a map and information in English and Italian, available from Como tourist office.

stupendous views of the lake and Alps. It's an ideal place for a picnic. From lungolargo Mazzoni, walk through piazza Mazzoni, to the entrance of Villa Serbelloni, turn right into via Roma then left onto via E Vitali and follow it to the end. If you're staying overnight, save your stroll for sunset or sunrise.

Centro storico Bellagio is tiny, just ten little streets lengthways, from the Parco Comunale in the south to Villa Serbelloni in the north, and only three small blocks wide at its most concentrated northern half – so it won't take you more than an hour to explore. Start at piazza Mazzoni on the waterfront with its elegant arcades with flowing drapes, then zig-zag your way up and down the stepped cobblestone streets, working your way from one end to the other. There are a surprising number of little stores to detain you, and even if you're not a shopper, you'll be charmed by the delightful buildings lining the narrow lanes with geranium-filled window boxes and bougainvillea tumbling down their walls. Specialties are Como's **famous silk** (Pierangelo Masciadri, salita Mella 19), **handmade glassware** (I Vetri di Bellagio, via Garibaldi 41 and 60), and **handcrafted wood** (Luigi Tacchi, via Garibaldi 22). There are some spots you shouldn't miss for their atmospheric antique interiors alone, including Bar Café Rossi (piazza Mazzini 22) and Enoteca Cava Turaccilio (salita Genazzini).

If you're not checking into the grand lakeside hotel **Villa Serbelloni** ⓘ *Via Roma 1, Bellagio, T031-950216, www.villaserbelloni.com,* or dining at its Michelin-starred restaurant, then at least soak up some old-world atmosphere. Stick your head in and ask nicely if you can see the sweeping staircases, sumptuous salons (where a pianist plays in the evenings) and breakfast room dripping with chandeliers. While there, book a guided walking tour (90 minutes; Tuesday to Sunday 1100 and 1530) through the villa's gorgeous 18th-century gardens sprawled on the wooded slopes above the village. The tour takes you on an amble through the park and a hike up to the ruins on the hilltop for arresting lake vistas. Apart from being a stunning setting, the place oozes history – it once belonged to Pliny the Elder!

A 10-minute stroll along the lungolargo to via P Carcano, in the direction of Como, will bring you to the marvellous gardens of the **Villa Melzi** ⓘ *Lungolario Marconi, T0339-457 3838, www.giardinidivillamelzi.it, Apr-Oct 0930-1830, guided tours €650,* once the residence of Duke of Lodi, Francesco Melzi d'Eril, vice-president of Napoleon's Italian republic. The neoclassical mansion was built between 1808 and 1810 and its clean, sober lines allow the eyes to take in the gorgeous countryside and lovely gardens which sprawl along the shoreline. Designed by architect Luigi Canonica and botanist Luigi Villoresi, who were responsible for Villa Reale north of Milan, the beautiful English gardens are dotted with sculptures, while the villa itself is also decorated with paintings and sculptures by some of the most famous artists of the time, including Antonio Canova. The Orangerie, once a greenhouse, is a tiny museum displaying objects from the Napoleonic period, including a bust of Napoleon and the keys to the city of Milan. Highlights include the Japanese gardens with ponds of water lilies, and a white and blue-tiled Moorish pavilion by the water.

Few foreign travellers explore the northern tip of Lake Como. **Gravedona** has an old medieval centre and 12th-century Santa Maria del Tiglio church, and nearby at **Domaso**, there's good windsurfing. **Colico** is an industrial town with little to interest travellers apart from its 11th-century abbey, the Abbazia di Piona. **Bellano** is also industrial, the centre for silk and cotton manufacturing, but it has a charming *centro storico*.

Varenna

Varenna is not as lively as the towns on Como's western shore, even at the height of summer – there are few shops, restaurants or cafés to kick back in – and while it's picturesque, it doesn't come close to Bellagio in terms of beauty. Its main square, piazza San Giorgio, is dominated by an imposing 10th-century Romanesque church, but it's now become a car park, and while there are a couple of cafés, they're not the kind of places you want to linger – unless your idea of amusement is watching people squeeze their small cars into miniscule spaces. There's another piazza near the ferry dock from where a waterside promenade takes you on a stroll by boats and ducks and fish swimming about.

Varenna's setting is splendid, however, with a steep mountain providing a dramatic backdrop and the lemon, ochre, salmon and russet buildings colour-coordinating beautifully. Its location opposite Menaggio, midway along the eastern shore between Lecco and the little-visited northern lake area, makes it a handy base for exploring the lake by boat. And for many, the dearth of attractions – it's eerily quiet at night – are its very appeal.

The village's main sight is Villa Monastero, but there's little else to do other than wander the skinny alleys tucked behind the bold villas lining the shore. A stroll will take all of half an hour but explore soon after dawn or just before dusk, and you'll enjoy some brilliant photo opportunities.

You'll also get great views on a hike up the hill behind Varenna on some occasionally precipitous stairs to the ruined medieval **Castello di Vezio** ① *Perledo, T0333-4485975, www.castellodivezio.it, Apr-Oct 1000-sunset, closed when raining, €4,* set amid olive groves, where the Lombard Queen Theodolinda died in the seventh century. If you're lucky you might get to see a bird of prey demonstration by the castle's falconer who cares for an impressive collection.

A lot less tourist-focused than the other villas on the lake, and more interested in its income from conferences and film shoots, **Villa Monastero** ① *Via IV Novembre, T0341-295450, www.villamonastero.eu, Mar-May and Sep-Oct Mon-Fri 0900-1300 and 1400-1800 (gardens only), villa museum and gardens Sat, Sun and holidays 0900-1300 and 1400-1800; Jun and Aug Mon-Thu 0900-1900 and Fri 0900-1300 (gardens only), villa museum and gardens Fri 1400-1900 and Sat, Sun and holidays 0900-1900. Garden only €5, garden and house museum €8,* is nevertheless worth a look if you're lucky enough to find it open. A former Cistercian convent, founded in 1208 by followers of Saint Mary Magdalena from Comacina Island, but was closed in the 16th century by San Carlo Borromeo due to the nun's rather licentious behaviour. While the villa's rooms are furnished with antiques and artistic treasures, the highlights are the perfumed gardens with their panoramic lake views, pretty waterfront pathways, and elegant loggias that frame the lake.

Lecco

Mark Twain wrote in *Innocents Abroad* of the 'wild mountain scenery' he enjoyed on his steamer voyage down the Lago di Lecco (the name given to this branch of Lake Como from Bellagio and Varenna south to Lecco) and of 'the towering cliffs on our left, and the pretty Lago di Lecco on our right'. Lecco's setting is one of the most dramatic on the lake, best appreciated by boat or on a stroll along the attractive waterfront.

Apart from these two assets, there's little to hold your interest here for longer than an hour or two, unless you're a fan of Lecco's favourite son and Italy's beloved novelist, Alessandro Manzoni (see page 26). In that case, you may want to see the author's statue on the main square and visit the house where the writer lived, **Villa Manzoni** ① *via Guanella 7, T0341-481247, Tue-Sun 0930-1730, €5*, which now comes under the umbrella of the **Musei Civici di Lecco** ① *www.museilecco.org*, and also houses the **Galleria Comunale d'Arte** and **Fototeca**, while several more museums are located at **Palazzo Belgiojoso** ① *corso Matteotti 32, T0341-481248, 0930-1400, €3*, including the **Museo Archeologico**, **Museo Storico** and **Museo di Storia Naturale**. Unless you're a real lover of museums, you'll be more than satisfied with a visit to Villa Manzoni, where the Fototeca features some stunning old black and white archival images of Lecco and surrounds.

Lake Como listings

For hotel and restaurant price codes and other relevant information, see pages 10-13.

◯ Where to stay

The lakes are generally seen as a summer destination, so many of these hotels (and their restaurants) close completely in winter, opening again around end of Mar.

Como *p60, map p64*

€€€ Albergo Terminus, Lungo Lario Trieste 14, T031-329111, www.albergo terminus.com. The pick of the bunch of Como's endearingly old-fashioned hotels, this 19th-century property overlooking the lake has contemporary rooms that sympathize with the older, classical decor of the rest of the hotel. For a unique experience, there's a delightful (albeit snug) room in the tower with French windows and lake views.

€€€ Barchetta Excelsior, Piazza Cavour 1, T031-3221, www.hotelbarchetta.it. With a brilliant location as the trump card, the chintzy feel of the rooms is easily forgiven if you're in one of the superior rooms with good views, or the suites – but in high season you'll certainly know you're paying for it.

€€€ Palace, Lungo Lario Trieste 16, T031-23391, www.palacehotel.it. Run by the same folks as the **Barchetta Excelsior**, this imposing hotel has 100 rooms, with many of the standard rooms facing the Duomo. Most superior rooms have lake views, but the deluxe rooms are a cert. A good breakfast, decent internet and secure parking.

€€ Due Corti, Piazza Vittoria 12/13, T031-328111, www.hotelduecorti.com. While not in the *centro storico*, nor overlooking the lake, this comfortable hotel in a renovated old pink building just outside the pedestrianized old town is still handily placed for sightseeing. Rooms are overpriced during summer, but the rest of the year they're a bargain.

€€ Tre Re, Via Boldoni 20, T031-265374, www.hoteltrere.com. This family-run hotel is a good, honest and spacious 3-star in a great location near the Duomo. Despite the classic exterior, the 40 hotel rooms are quite modern (some have balconies) and the hotel has parking. Decent restaurant attached to the hotel as well.

€€ Villa Flori, Via Cernobbio 12, T031-33820, www.hotelvillaflori.com. A gracious 45-room hotel (many with a terrace overlooking the lake), this was once an exquisite villa that became a hotel in 1958. The romantic Garibaldi suite is where the famous Italian hero spent the first night of his honeymoon; however, the marriage didn't last long – it appears that his young bride, Giuseppina Raimondi, was experienced beyond her years…

€ Albergo Del Duca, Piazza Mazzini 12, T031-264859, www.albergodelduca.it. A renovated 17th-century villa, this hotel's rooms have wooden floorboards and exposed beams and are clean and simple. A great location makes it an excellent budget choice in Como. There's parking, but let them know in advance.

€ Quarcino, Salita Quarcino 4, T031-303934, www.hotelquarcino.it. Another simple, clean and inexpensive choice in a town not known for great value, **Hotel Quarcino** has good facilities for the price, including Wi-Fi. Private parking is available.

Cernobbio *p64*

€€€€ Villa d'Este, Via Regina 40, T031-3481, www.villadeste.it. **Villa d'Este** is a lavish hotel with sprawling lawns and a prime lakeside location that's the envy of other properties in the region. The 17th-century hotel has had many a famous face wander its whimsical gardens, and while the character-filled rooms have their own idiosyncrasies, this is the kind of hotel where you let romance dictate your stay. If you're staying at the height of summer, book hotel restaurants in advance and raise your credit card limit.

Tremezzo p66

€€€ Grand Hotel Tremezzo, Via Regina 8, T034-442491, www.grandhoteltremezzo. com. Close to the delightful **Villa Carlotta**, this grand hotel, dating to 1910, is sumptuously appointed, with excellent dining and service. The rooms, superior level and above, have brilliant lake views, while the classic rooms face the garden. All are beautifully decorated with period furniture and fittings. Both indoor and outdoor pools are a treat.

Bellagio p67

€€€ Grand Hotel Villa Serbelloni, Via Roma 1, T031-950216, www.villaserbelloni. com. One of the oldest lake hotels, **Villa Serbelloni** offers up the quintessential Como experience. The handsome old place exudes atmosphere, from the gilt-edged mirrors and chandeliered high ceilings to the gigantic lakeside pool. There are verdant grounds to explore and elegant restaurants to dress up for (one with a Michelin star, **Mistral**, see page 75). Book a room with a view.

€€ Du Lac, Piazza Mazzini 32, T031-950320, www.bellagiohoteldulac.com. Smack bang in the town centre, this family-run hotel might be a little old-fashioned, but the views from the upper floors (ask for a lake view room on the fourth) make up for it. Check out the wonderful rooftop terrace.

€€ Suisse, Piazza Mazzini 8, T031-951755, www.bellagio.co.nz/Suisse. This small, simple, 10-room hotel above the **Ristorante Albergo Suisse** is a pretty good deal for Bellagio, as is their restaurant.

❼ Restaurants

Regional dishes, delicious seafood and great wines await, but make sure that the restaurant of your desires is open – opening times vary, although most open for lunch (1200-1500) and dinner (1900-2300) at least 6 days and nights a week. Keep in mind that

most Lakes restaurants close Dec-Jan, some staying shut as late as Mar, and some also close 1 night a week, generally Mon or Tue.

Como p60, map p64

€€ Bar Del Terme, Restaurant at Albergo Terminus, Lungo Lario Trieste 14, T031-329111, www.albergoterminus.com. An elegant little restaurant set in the equally elegant **Albergo Terminus**, it's a romantic spot for dinner. The cuisine is classic Italian, but with all the usual dishes handled with exquisite care and presented beautifully – try their handmade pastas.

€€ Il Pinzimonio, Via Bonanomi 24, T031-268667, www.il-pinzimonio.it. Set in a historic building in the heart of the centre, the playful contemporary decor melds old wooden beams, exposed stone, brick walls and rustic flowerboxes with contemporary minimalist Italian design. The food equally and effortlessly combines classics with modern interpretations. Locals love the pizzas.

€€ Il Solito Posto, Via Lambertenghi 9, T031-271352, www.ilsolitoposto.net. The warm glow of lights within beckon customers from beneath the vine-covered entrance at this restaurant on a quiet cobbled lane. Once inside the cosy interior, complete with fireplace, it's hard to leave. The focus is on classic hearty cuisine such as *tagliolini al ragu di coniglio* (pasta with rabbit sauce) and *risotto gamberi e zucchini* (risotto with prawns and zucchini). The 2-course set lunch menu is popular.

€€ Il Vecchio Borgo, Piazza Matteotti 1, T031-304522, www.ilvecchioborgocomo.it. A good choice when some in your group just want a simple pizza and others some grilled fish or seafood pasta. They do excellent Italian classics, but the local lake seafood – especially the perch – is worth sampling.

€€ Joy, Via Cernobbio 2, T031-572132, www.joyrestaurant.it. With its funky purple interior, big wooden deck with brilliant panoramic vistas of the lake, and great pizzas and pastas, this chic casual eatery is currently the local favourite – and it's well off the tourist trail.

€€ L'Antica Riva, Lungo Lario Trieste 50, T031-305221, www.anticariva.it. Lake Como is a great place to try seafood and this popular restaurant delivers with excellent seafood platters, sublime carpaccio of tuna, and delicious seafood pastas. Excellent lakeside location.

€€ Le Soste Ristorante, Via A Diaz 52A, T031-266024. Closed Sun. Save this elegant restaurant and equally refined cuisine for an evening meal, when you can take your time enjoying the deliciously simple food, from smoked goose breast served with brioche, foie gras and apple puree, to *gnocchi di patate con burro montate e semi di papavero* (potato dumplings with melted butter and poppy seeds).

€€ Raimondi, Hotel Villa Flori, via Cernobbio 12, T031-33820, www.hotel villaflori.com. With an unbeatable location and a terrace hovering gracefully over the lake, it's the perfect place to try some lake fish – one of the dishes that makes the locals return time and again. Other Italian classics are treated with equal care.

€ Il Carrettiere, Via Coloniola 18, T031-303478, www.ilcarrettiere.eu. Locals love this restaurant for its honest, home-style Sicilian fare and warm ambiance. Tucked away on a back street behind the lake, the wood-fired pizzas are superb and the mixed seafood (*fritto misto*) just one of the excellent seafood dishes on the menu.

€ Pizzeria La Darsena, Lungo Lario Trieste 54, T031-301081, www.la-darsena.it. Next door to L'Antica Riva, Pizzeria La Darsena is the place to come when you're not in the mood for fuss, and don't want to spend much, yet you still want a lake view – admittedly, overlooking the road too. The pizzas are very good.

€ Riva Café, Via Cairoli 10, T031-264325. This buzzy pizzeria in a sleek contemporary style (cream leather, slate floor, chocolate wood) might not appeal to those looking for the quintessential lakeside restaurant, but

it's popular with locals who come for the 70 types of pizza, from classics to unusual topping combinations, such as salmon, rocket, gorgonzola and walnuts – delicious!

Cafés

Caffè Alessandro Volta, Piazza A Volta. Named after the Como-born physicist and inventor of the battery, Alessandro Volta (born 1745), this simple café with an alfresco terrace and stand-up bar inside is enormously popular with locals.

Caffè Nova Comum, Piazza Duomo 2, T031-260483. Popular with locals and tourists alike, the views of Como's striped cathedral don't get much better than from the alfresco terrace of this old-fashioned café. Locals head here for cappuccino for breakfast or a prosecco in the afternoon, while tourists fill up on the fresh panini.

Gelateria Ceccato, Lungo Lario Trieste 16, next to the Palace Hotel Lake Como. Situated in an elegant building opposite the waterfront, this gelateria is easily Como's most popular – just look for the people spilling out onto the street on a summer's evening. There's an alfresco area upstairs with pretty iron lacework overlooking the lake; however, locals prefer to stroll by the water while they do their licking.

Menaggio *p66*

€€ Le Tout Paris, Lungolago Castelli 9, Grand Hotel Victoria, T03-443 2003. With its crisp white linen tablecloths and flower arrangements, this is a very elegant restaurant serving up reasonably priced regional and Italian classics. The location opposite the waterfront makes it a romantic spot – especially if the musicians are playing.

Bellagio *p67*

€€ Mistral, restaurant at Grand Hotel Villa Serbelloni, via Roma 1, T031-950216, www. villaserbelloni.com. Hotel Villa Serbelloni is doubly blessed, with Michelin-starred chef Ettore Bocchia watching over both restaurants in the hotel. However, it's his

Mistral restaurant where Bocchia spreads his gastronomic wings. **Mistral** is his laboratory of molecular gastronomy and even though Bocchia isn't afraid of culinary fireworks and flashy presentation, the flavour is firmly on the plate – right up to his innovative gelato!

€€ Ristorante Barchetta, Salita Mella 13, T031-951389, www.ristorantebarchetta. com. Book ahead for this wildly popular restaurant – locals are either dining here themselves or sending guests here. Fish fresh from the lake is a favourite (try the local perch) and the meat dishes excellent for those who have had their fill of seafood.

€ La Grotta, Salita Cernaia 14, T031-951152. Another local favourite, this comfy and welcoming restaurant does a roaring trade with its excellent thin pizzas (try the one with capers and anchovies) and fish main courses.

Varenna *p71*

€€ Vecchia Varenna, Contrada Scoscesa 10, T03-4183 0793, www.vecchiavarenna.it. **Vecchia Varenna** is widely considered to be one of the most romantic restaurants on the lake – if you're a couple book for dinner, otherwise a relaxing (long) lunch here is recommended for the excellent fresh seafood and calming lake views.

Lecco *p71*

€€ Nicolin, Via Ponchielli 54, T03-4142 2122. This homely, inviting, family-run restaurant has lovely garden seating in summer and a fine wine list. The food is classic northern Italian with the occasional imaginative twist.

Bars and clubs

The thing to do on Lake Como, and it doesn't matter which part of the lake you're on, is to have a late afternoon aperitivo and nibbles (generally a few small dishes of chips, nuts and olives) at a waterfront café-bar. After dinner, head to the nearest gelateria to buy a gelato and take a saunter along the water's edge.

Bars

Café-bars are located on the waterfront at Como and the towns and villages all around the lake, as well as lining the perimeters of most piazzas. Most of the bars doubling as cafés open all day, from morning until fairly late at night, and might close 1 day a week (often Mon). Bars that mainly serve as wine bars tend to open around lunch and close after midnight. Como has the most interesting bars and a fairly lively bar scene compared to the other towns, while Bellagio's waterfront bar-cafés are probably the most romantic for a pre- or post-dinner drink. During summer, some of the villa gardens, such as **Villa del Balbianello** (see page 65), host happy hours (generally from 1830-2030) which will feature an alfresco cocktail bar and live jazz or other music.

Al Molo, Lungo Lario Trieste, Como (opposite the Stazione Nord train terminus). Little more than a stand-up bar with a handful of tables and chairs outside covered in red-checked tablecloths, Al Molo boasts one of Como's best locations for sunset-watching with a glass of something in hand. Little dishes of snacks are also served during aperitivo hour. It may not be flash but this is the kind of place you can settle in for a while.

Mesa Redonda, Via A Diaz 28, Como. The red country'n'western-style typeface on the black portico may seem out of place in Como's elegant old town, and this dark bar may seem an odd fit too, but it's hugely popular with young arty types, especially late on a weekend night; by day anybody and everybody drops in for a drink.

Osteria del Gallo, Via Vitani 16, Como, T031-270279. Look for the delightfully old-fashioned *osteria* sign above the arched doors to find this atmospheric wine bar, a favourite with locals, which serves a good selection of local wines alongside plates of cold cuts and cheeses.

♦ Shopping

Most shops on Lake Como open from Mon-Sat 0930 or 1000, close for lunch at 1200 or 1300, then reopen from 1600-1900, although in Como town and Bellagio many shops stay open all day, especially throughout the busy summer tourist season. You'll find the most sophisticated shopping at Como and Bellagio, where the cobblestone streets are crammed with chic boutiques selling fashion, jewellery, shoes and handbags, and shops specializing in Italian crafts and souvenirs, including hand-painted ceramics, pottery and glassware, as well as gourmet food and wine.

Lake Como is famous for its silk, and Como and Bellagio are the best places to shop for silk scarves, shawls, foulards, cravats and ties. In Como, **A Picci** (via Vittorio Emanuele 54, T031-261369) is a well-regarded, old-fashioned store stocking fine quality classic pieces, while in Bellagio, **Pierangelo Masciadri** (salita Mella 19, T031-950067, www.masciadri.tv), a Brera Academy graduate (see page 36), creates beautiful silk creations using his own prints with designs inspired by history, art and architecture; his shop displays photos of the rich and famous who have come here to buy his products.

♦ What to do

Lakes excursions and cruises
Via per Cernobbio 18, Como, T031-579211, www.navigazionelaghi.it. The government-operated water transport service for Lake Como offers frequent services from Como to various towns, villages and sights around the lake, including Cernobbio, Colico, Argegno, Lenno, Tremezzo, Villa Carlotta, Bellagio, Menaggio, Varenna, Bellano, Gravedona, and Lecco, on several different types of boat: *servizio rapido* (fast catamaran), *servizio*

autotraghetto (a slower ferry), and *corso battello* (an even slower 'ship'). During summer, there are also daily excursions and themed cruises (€15-22), some of which offer lunch and dinner (€15-19).
Rent A Boat, various marinas and docks around Lake Como, T038-0843 5253, www.rentland.it. You can rent easy-to-drive speed boats, water skis, wake boards and wetsuits, from 1 hr to 1 week, from a number of marinas and docks around the lake. Call to find the nearest location to where you're staying. Prices range from €65 per hr and €2,200 for 12 days.
Seaplane Tours, Aero Club Como, viale Masia 44, Como, T031-574495, www.aero clubcomo.com. Probably the most popular activity to do on the lake is to take a scenic flight on a sea plane. This company has been offering flights since 1930 and has an excellent reputation.

Language
Inlingua, Via Luini 3, Como, T031-431 0092, www.inlingua.it. This highly regarded Italian language school, in operation for 30 years, offers packages of 10 lessons over 1, 2 or 3-day periods, aimed at foreigners on holidays. You can arrange 1-on-1 lessons, or in pairs, or small groups of 5 people.

Sport and outdoor
For watersports such as sailing, windsurfing and kayaking, and outdoor activities including mountain biking and rides on the Brunate funicular, see box, page 68.

♦ Directory

Hospital Ospedale Generale Di Zona Valduce, via Dante Alighieri 11, T031-324111. **Pharmacy** Farmacia Centrale, caio Plinio Secondo 1 (off piazza Cavour), T031-304204, Mon 1530-1930, Tue-Sun 0830-1230 and 1530-1930

Lake Maggiore and Lake Orta

The grandest of all the lakes, Lago Maggiore is also one of the more peaceful lakes, lacking the development that sometimes conspires to spoil the Lake Garda experience. The highlight is no doubt the triplet of atmospheric islands owned by the influential Borromeo dynasty, with Isola Bella and its palatial grounds a breathtakingly beautiful sight and one full of history.

Most foreign travellers visiting Lake Maggiore make their base on the western shore, at one of three places. Stresa is an elegant, albeit faded fin-de-siècle resort with a maze of pedestrianized streets and charming buildings. The pretty town of Verbania across the water has a lively waterfront lined with lovely emerald parks. Both towns come to life on their weekly market days. Charming Cannobio further upstream has colourful old buildings skirting a charismatic waterfront lined with alfresco cafés, while the steep lanes leading off the waterfront are also enigmatic. Its small lakeside beach sees the locals sunbathing on the lawn beside the town promenade during summer, while the foreign visitors look on in bemusement.

Petite and picturesque Lake Orta is arguably the most alluring of all the lakes in northern Italy. Popular with wealthy Italians and northern Europeans, the lakeside village of Orta San Giuilo is pretty as a postcard and if a little touristy during the middle of the day, it's enchanting by the late afternoon when everyone is out for a stroll. Opposite, the island of Isola di San Giulio, with the splendid Basilica of St Giulio, is a highlight of these lakes.

Stresa → For listings, see pages 86-92.

The grande dame of lake resorts, Stresa has been a popular holiday spot since Napoleon carved a route through the mountains in the early 19th century, and the Simplon tunnel and railway line opened the way for the Grand Tour travellers heading south (see box, page 98). Two centuries later and tourists are still flocking here, but while the Stresa that Stendhal, Dickens and Byron waxed lyrical about has long gone, the place still has a certain retro-charm and undeniable allure – largely due to its grand old hotels, temperate Mediterranean climate, and an archipelago of lovely islands off-shore.

Boasting pastel buildings and pretty piazzas where people linger at alfresco cafés to eat enormous dishes of gelato, Stresa is still an undeniably attractive town – in spite of the traffic, tacky souvenir shops and hordes of tourists in summer. Pass through in winter when the hotels are closed up and the craggy limestone mountains appear even more dramatic blanketed in snow, and you can better picture the tranquil, isolated place that has inspired poets and writers (after visiting in 1948 Ernest Hemingway set part of *A Farewell to Arms* at the Grand Hotel des Iles Borromees) and drew aristocrats to build elegant villas here. Villa Pallavicino can be visited, and indeed, apart from strolling Stresa's picturesque lakeside promenade, lined with vibrant-coloured flowerbeds, visiting the luxuriant Borromeo islands, and taking a hike up **Monte Mottarone** (see page 92), there's little else to do but explore the gracious villa and its fragrant gardens. There is a **tourist information office** ① *Piazza Marconi 16, T0323-30150, www.distrettolaghi.it, Mar-Oct daily 1000-1230 and 1500-1830, Nov-Feb Mon-Fri only.*

Villa Pallavicino

① *Via Sempione Sud 8, Stresa, T0323-31533, www.parcozoopallavicino.it, Mar-Oct, daily 0900-1800, €9.50/€6.50 4-12.*

These splendid villa grounds near the lake were opened to the public after the Second World War. The villa sits atop a hill with distant views of the eastern shore of Lake Maggiore. There's an abundance of flora, animals and birdlife in the lush 20-ha botanical gardens and zoo, including peacocks and ostriches that roam at will, and a wonderful park with picnic areas, a café-bar and a playground for the kids.

Borromean Islands

① *www.isoleborromee. Isola Bella and Isola Madre: end Mar-Oct, daily 0900-1730; Isola Bella €13, Isola Madre €11, combined ticket €18. Isola Bella Pinacoteca: daily 0900-1300 and 1330-1700, €4. Guided island visits (booking essential) €45, T0331-931300 or online. Boat services to the islands are operated by Navigazione Lago Maggiore (T0322-233200, navigazionelaghi.it) but don't panic if you miss a boat or you decide to spend longer on one island as there are also private boatmen on all of the islands.*

The bewitching Borromean Islands, situated just off Stresa on Lake Maggiore's western shore, are arguably the most enchanting of any on the lakes. The islands are owned by the Borromeo family (see box, page 81), who started buying them up in the 16th century. A day spent hopping between them by boat, exploring their beautifully landscaped gardens and gracious *palazzi* and enjoying the gorgeous vistas is an absolute delight. Especially when punctuated by a sublime seafood lunch!

There are three islands: **Isola Bella** (the beautiful island), **Isola dei Pescatori** (the island of fishermen, also called Isola Superiore), and **Isola Madre** (the mother island), the largest. It makes most sense to visit them in this order, but if you want a full day exploring and don't want to rush around, then you'll need to catch the earliest boat you can from Stresa. Note that you need to buy your tickets for entry to the island's museums and villas when you buy your boat tickets at the Stresa dock.

Isola Bella, named after Countess Isabella Borromeo, boasts a sumptuous baroque summer palace and stunning terraced gardens. The richly decorated palace, which Count Vitaliano Borromeo began building in 1632, is now a Pinacoteca (art gallery) with priceless paintings, sculptures, antique furniture and tapestries on display; however, it's the gardens that most people come to see.

Considered to be a fine example of the 17th-century Italian garden style, they have ornate arrangements of flowers and plants set out on overlapping terraces (10 in all!), all carefully selected to ensure something is always in bloom from spring to autumn. Don't miss the chapel with the family tombs and the quirky mosaic grotto. Allow one or two hours to see the palace and gardens; picnics aren't allowed so you probably won't feel the need to stay any longer.

Isola dei Pescatori, said to be a favourite spot of Hemingway's, is tiny – just 90 m wide and 500 m long – yet it's a busy little fishing village of an island, where fishermen still live and work. Wander the lanes first (it won't take long) where you'll find Madonnas in shrines (to protect the fishermen) and nets strewn about the place. There are a handful of excellent seafood restaurants, which makes it a great place to stop for lunch.

The largest island, **Isola Madre**, boasts the most luxuriant gardens of all. Nicknamed the 'Botanical Island', it's home to an array of exotic plants and flowers, including the biggest kashmir cypress tree in Europe. The island also boasts an elegant villa which can be explored, with plush furnishings and paintings, and – the highlight for many – an enormous room-size puppet theatre with elaborately painted sets, beautifully made marionettes, and various bits and pieces of puppet paraphernalia on display.

But once again, it's the glorious gardens that most come for – these ones boasting dense forest with shaded paths and fine lake views, exotic palm trees and towering cacti, and whatever time of year you visit, flowers cascading all about the place. For garden enthusiasts the times to visit are April for the camellias and May for the azaleas and rhododendrons, although you're guaranteed to find something blooming throughout the year.

The Borromeo family

An important and influential family throughout Milan's history has been the Borromeo family, but their rise to prominence only came after the death of the head of the family, Filippo, who was decapitated by the Florentines after a revolt in 1370, his children having fled to Milan. Once the family became established in Milan, Vitaliano I (c 1391–1449) put in place the foundations of what was to become a great legacy. Vitaliano, due to his savvy business dealings, purchased the family's first land near Lake Maggiore. The next major player in the family was Giberto II (c 1511-1558) who, as a cardinal, strengthened the family image. But it wasn't until the next generation that the family's name was cemented in history.

Carlo Borromeo (1538-1584) became a very popular Reformist archbishop in 1564 and after his death his cousin Federico (1564-1631) worked tirelessly to have his cousin canonized, which he eventually succeeded in doing in 1610. In 1593 Federico had been made a cardinal and went on to become archbishop of Milan in 1595 and continued the reforms initiated by his cousin. He notably set up the Biblioteca Ambrosiana and its gallery in Milan (see page 23). The family continued its good work and good fortune under Carlo III (1586-1652), the nephew and heir of Cardinal Federico. Today the dynasty still survives and the interests of the family are concentrated on preserving their heritage.

Verbania → *For listings, see pages 86-92.*

Verbania, like its neighbour Stresa across the Gulf of Pallanza, is all about the waterfront, with a picturesque promenade around the promontory that's a fine place for a stroll, particularly on balmy summer evenings. Like Stresa, Verbania has a long history of tourism, with its piazzas lined with alfresco cafes and gelaterias, crammed with postcard stands, and uncomfortably crowded with people in high summer. It also sports what the 19th-century travel writers who visited might have called 'gaily painted' buildings. Decorated with flowerboxes and bold awnings, the gelato-coloured edifices have a quaint charm very different to the grandeur and splendour of Stresa. But like its neighbour, Verbania – actually three towns in one, Suna, Intra and Pallanza (Mussolini named them all 'Verbania' in 1939) – has its fair share of gracious villas with luxuriant gardens, the most famous of which is Villa Taranto.

Giardini Botanici Villa Taranto
ⓘ *Pallanza, T0323-556667, www.villataranto.it, daily Mar-Sep 0830-1830, Oct 0830-1700, €10/€5.50 6-14.*

Boasting verdant terraces dotted with waterfalls, fountains, and pools floating with lilies, these botanical gardens on the Pallanza promontory are simply bewitching. If there's one local attraction you shouldn't miss, it's this lifetime labour of love of intriguing Scotsman Captain Neil Boyd McEacharn. Born in 1884 to an affluent shipping and mining family with business interests in Australia, McEacharn visited Italy as a child, an experience that forever changed the life of this member of the Royal Company of Archers, who decided to pursue his passion for botany. Travelling to Italy in 1928 to source land to establish a research garden, McEacharn purchased La Crocetta from the Marquise of Sant'Elia, and began planting the 16 acres of land with seeds and plants from around the world. Forced to leave during the Second World War, he gifted the Italian State his garden on the condition it remained private, and set sail for Australia. Returning after the war, McEacharn was begged by the Italians to open the gates to the public, which he did in 1952. In return, he was honoured with the keys to the city in 1963. The Captain died a year later at his villa on a veranda overlooking the stunning views of his garden.

McEacharn's garden is much admired for its combination of wild beauty and elegant symmetry – the result of his blending of natural English Romantic garden and the classic Italian style based on formal terraces and geometric patterns – but also his decades-long efforts to establish the garden on chestnut fields. With more than 8500 plant varieties, including rare specimens collected from around the globe, and acclimatized over long periods, it's a superb example of a botanic garden where plants are settled into microclimates. Highlights include the dahlia gardens (with over 300 varieties), avenues of azaleas, maple, rhododendron and camellia, carpets of heathers, greenhouse treasures, including the enormous Victoria amazonica, and rare lilies. All plants are labelled; you can also buy a guidebook at the entrance and follow the numbered arrows. Allow an hour or so to stroll the gardens.

Stops on the Lake Maggiore circuit

If you're driving a circuit of Lake Maggiore, as many people do, head south from Stresa along the western shore to Arona, then loop around to the eastern shore and head north to Locarno, Switzerland, returning south on the western shore via Cannobio and Verbania. The drive alone will take half a day; however, it can stretch to a full day with the following detours along the way:

Start by driving to **Arona**, 17 km south of Stresa. A Borromeo dynasty stronghold before Napoleon arrived, Arona is famous for its gigantic 17th-century bronze statue of Carlo Borromeo (you can climb inside and look out his pupils).

Drive on to the Borromeos' medieval castle, **Rocca di Angera** ① *T0331-931300, daily 0900-1730, €7*, 16 km northeast from Arona, on the opposite shore from Stresa. It has frescoes in the Sala della Giustizia dating to 1342 (some of Lombardy's oldest) a splendid tower with fabulous lake vistas, and a doll museum.

Santa Caterina del Sasso ① *Mar-Oct daily 0830-1200 and 1430-1800, Nov-Feb weekends only, free*, 15 km north from Rocca di Angera, is your next stop. There are 12th-century frescoes inside but it's the dramatic setting of this monastic complex, built into a cliff face, that people marvel at.

Sitting 60 km further north, in Switzerland, are **Locarno and Ascona**. Locarno's modern glass buildings obscure a medieval centre that's worth seeking out, especially the 14th-century Castello Visconteo, while neighbouring Ascona, once an artists' haunt, has streets lined with chic boutiques.

Finally, crossing back to Italy is **Cannero Riviera** ① *23 km south*. With its hilly lanes, vivid houses, bougainvillea and fruit trees, Cannero has Mediterranean ambiance that makes it a pleasure to explore. Don't miss the little castle islands off shore. From Cannero Riviera, the drive south to Stresa is 30 km and takes around 40 minutes.

Take a drive from Cannobio

If you're keen to get your head in the clouds and inhale some fresh mountain air, there's a wonderful drive to do from Cannobio that encircles the **Parco Nazionale della Val Grande** (Great Valley National Park) in Piedmont. The park itself is not easy to explore unless you slip on some skis (during winter) or take a hike (during the warmer months), best organized with a guide through one of the tourist offices. But you can enjoy the craggy mountains of the park from the comfort of your car, and punctuate the journey with invigorating walks along the way. In spring, the velvety meadows are blanketed with wildflowers and in autumn, the trees are all shades of brown and gold. Take extra caution on this route during summer when every cyclist in Italy seems to be out on the roads.

From the southern side of Cannobio, take the turn-off west, signposted with a brown tourist marker saying 'Val Cannobio'. You won't miss it but if you do, there's another road on the northern side of town also heading west that meets up with it. The moment you

get off the main road, you'll notice the landscape change immediately as you quickly ascend along narrow winding roads, crawling across old stone arched bridges, through lush dense forest to high mountainous wilderness. The slender road trims right down to a thin stick of a lane in parts where it can be near impossible to pass other cars, so do take care, but for some this is part of the fun. If you see a spot to pull over, take it, as they're few and far between and getting out and stretching your legs as you breathe in the crisp air is glorious. After an hour or so hugging the hills and snaking through tunnels of trees, you'll join up to the main road at Malesco, and, if you're not careful, the freeway at Domodóssola. It's much more enjoyable to stick with the smaller roads though, even though they run right near the freeway, as these allow you to stop and explore the ruins of castle towers and churches. Otherwise, blink and you'll be back in Cannobio. You will come to Verbania first, or you can head south instead to Omegna and visit Lake Orta.

Cannobio → *For listings, see pages 86-92.*

Boasting a labyrinthine *centro storico* of medieval stone houses, elegant arcades, and skinny pebble streets that crawl down the hillside, Cannobio is the most charming town on Lake Maggiore. But it's the glimpses of cobalt water between the colourful old houses that line the lakefront and the alfresco cafés along the tranquil pedestrian-only waterside promenade that really make Cannobio captivating.

There's very little to actually do here but that's part of the charm of the place and what makes it a wonderful spot for a relaxing summer break. Locals spend their days sunbathing on the patch of grass that serves as a 'beach', while the teenagers dive from the concrete ruin that juts into the lake, and the older folk chat on the shady benches overlooking the sparkling water.

In the evening everyone comes out for the *passeggiatta* and *aperitivi* at the waterside bars, afterwards cramming the restaurant terraces for their fish meals, and then once again doing laps of the promenade with a gelato in hand. If you get bored with this, Verbania is a 30-minute drive south, and Switzerland 10 minutes north, or you can head up to the hills for some fresh mountain air (see box, above).

Lake Orta → *For listings, see pages 86-92.*

The most bewitching of all of Italy's northern lakes, Lake Orta is an absolute delight to explore. There is really only one place that makes an engaging base here and that's the delightful Orta San Giulio. If you drive around the lake, Omegna and Pella are worth a look, although the best part of the drive will be the views from Pella across to Isola di San Giulio. At the northern end of the lake, Omegna has an attractive canal and cafés opposite the waterfront that make a perfect lunch stop, while laid-back Pella, which sees few tourists stopping at all, has a pleasant café-bar on its lakefront.

Orta San Giulio
Visit once and you'll find yourself returning to this charismatic little medieval village with its captivating views of Isola di San Giulio (San Giulio Island) just offshore.

Splendidly situated on a tiny promontory jutting into the lake and surrounded by fragrant wooded forests and undulating emerald hills, Orta San Giulio boasts the most stunning setting of any village in the lakes region. It's also one of the quietest. Take a stroll around the tranquil lanes in the early morning or late afternoon and all you'll hear is silence. Add to the dramatic location a lake that is the deepest blue, traffic-free cobblestone streets lined with charming shops, gourmet grocery shops and alfresco cafés, and a mountain dotted with 21 chapels illustrating the life of Saint Francis of Assisi – the **Sacro Monte di San Francisco**, a UNESCO World Heritage Site – which serves as a backdrop.

There's no denying that Orta San Giulio is touristy – at the height of summer tour buses stream in, dropping their passengers at the tourist office to catch the road-train in, and nearly every shop sells useless trinkets and has a postcard stand. However, at the same time its diminutive size and gracious aristocratic villas give the village an air of exclusivity. As does enchanting **Villa Crespi**, a whimsical Moorish-inspired boutique hotel with a Michelin-starred restaurant. Visit in spring or autumn to enjoy the village at its most peaceful, when it will just be you and the locals sunning yourselves at a café, or reclined on one of the park benches watching the boats putter across to the island. There's a **tourist information office** ① *Via Panoramica, T0322-905614, www.distrettolaghi.eu.*

Isola di San Giulio
Named after fourth-century patron saint Julius of Novara, and once home to serpents and dragons according to local legend, Isola di San Giulio (San Giulio Island), offshore from Orta San Giulio, is easily one of the lakes' most alluring islets. Only 140 m wide and 275 m long, the island boasts one sight worth seeing – the **Basilica di Saint Giulio** ① *0930-1200 and 1400-1845, free,* with a splendid Romanesque tower, and adjoining it a whitewashed **Benedictine convent**. Dating to the 14th century, the church interior boasts vaulted ceilings and naïve frescoes that are worth a quick look, but it's just as enjoyable to wander the island's only street and do some reflection – as the multilingual signs the Benedictine nuns have erected suggest. Boats do the five-minute run from Orta's piazza Motta to the island every 15 minutes or when they're full; daily April to September, weekends October to November and March, stopping altogether December to February, €3 return.

Lake Maggiore and Lake Orta listings

For hotel and restaurant price codes and other relevant information, see pages 10-13.

🛏 Where to stay

The lakes are generally seen as a summer destination, so many of these hotels (and their restaurants) close completely in winter, opening again around end of Mar.

Stresa *p79*

€€€€ Grand Hotel des Iles Borromées, Corso Umberto I 67, T0323-938938, www. borromees.it. This belle époque masterpiece on a vast waterfront property is reason enough to stay in Stresa alone. Originally built in 1861 and exquisitely restored only a few years ago, it's lake opulence at its best, despite the fact that it's popular with groups and conferences. While a lake view room is the most romantic choice, the garden view rooms don't suffer from a lack of attention as they do in some other lakeside hotels. The main restaurant is a fine dining affair with formal dress expected in the evening. Yes, it's that kind of place.

€€€ Il Sole di Ranco, Piazza Venezia 5, Ranco, T0331-976507, www.ilsolediranco.it. This small hotel spread over 2 villas is renowned for the excellent cuisine of the Brovelli family who have been here on the lake for more than 150 years. While previously the food was the highlight, the rooms have been upgraded and are now worthy in supporting the creative cuisine of Davide Brovelli. It's a lovely spot to relax at and the hotel has views from the suites and a decent swimming pool to work off those calories.

€€ Residence La Luna Nel Porto, Corso Italia 60, T0323-934466, www. lalunanelporto.it. This cross between a hotel and studio apartments is best experienced for a week or more so you can settle in and enjoy the lakefront position. The spacious apartments have modern furnishings, excellent views and all facilities suitable for a long stay, including broadband internet. Shared kitchen facilities available.

Isola dei Pescatori

€€ Ristorante Verbano, Via Ugo Ara 2, T0323-30408, www.hotelverbano.it. The best value option here, this hotel has a wonderful, romantic atmosphere and a lovely garden restaurant. The rooms are cosy and have excellent views and it's a great place to hole up for a few days – but perhaps not during the height of the tourist season. It's a few mins by boat from Stresa.

Verbania *p82*

€€€€ Villa Claudia dei Marchesi Dal Pozzo, S Strada del Sempione 5, T0322-772011, www.villaclaudiadalpozzo.com. This property is actually 2 separate structures, the villa and the Borgo (longer-stay accommodation), dating from the 18th century; both overlook the lake. There are 6 suites available in the exclusive villa with period furniture and all mod cons (except air conditioning), while the comfy Borgo has 12 rooms with a/c and hot tubs. There is also a well-regarded bistro, if you find the premises too hard to leave.

€€ Pallanzo, Viale Magnolie 8, T0323-503202, www.pallanzahotels.com. A great location across from the ferry dock, this is a handsome art nouveau style 4-star hotel. There are 48 rooms, most with views and a variety of configurations and colour schemes, and all have air conditioning. They also have a good value 3-star hotel, the **Belvedere San Gottardo**.

Cannobio *p84*

€€ Cannobio, Piazza Vittorio Emanuele III 6, T0323-739639, www.hotelcannobio. com. This elegant hotel has one of the best locations in town, right on the waterfront (ask for a lake view room with balcony) overlooking the promenade. Private parking, a great breakfast, and fine alfresco restaurant.

There is a very appealing junior suite with a double balcony and jacuzzi.

€€ Pironi, Via Marconi 35, T0323-70624, www.pironihotel.it. This former 15th-century palace has had a thoughtful restoration and boasts original frescoes, vaulted ceilings, well-placed antiques and a beautiful breakfast room. There are 12 individually decorated rooms (some with lake views) and while it's not directly on the waterfront, the atmospheric medieval village setting is fitting.

€ Antica Stallera, Via P Zacchero 3, T0323-71595, www.anticastallera.com. This small hotel and restaurant has modern rooms with en suite and an attractive and well-regarded garden restaurant.

Orta San Giulio p85

€€€€ Villa Crespi, Via G Fava 18, Orta San Giulio, T0322-911902, www. hotelvillacrespi.it. If nothing else, the sight of Villa Crespi, a Moorish-style villa built in 1879, is a startling one. And if the idea of the Middle East adjacent to Lake Orta is fantastic, the exotic interior details keep the suspension of belief alive a little longer. 14 ornate rooms of varying size and detail are on offer, but topping the magical atmosphere is the cuisine of star chef Antonino Cannavacciuolo whose creativity outshines the whimsicality of the accommodation.

€€€ San Rocco, Via Gippini 11, T0322-911977, www.hotelsanrocco.it. A 4-star hotel with an enviable lake location, this is a popular retreat for honeymooners, with a spa, private swimming pool and lake views the main incentives. Over half the rooms have watery vistas but book early and reconfirm. While the decoration of the rooms in the old convent is fine, the 11 rooms in the villa are superb.

€€ Orta, Piazza Motta 1, T0322-90253, www.hotelorta.it. With a prime position right on the main square and overlooking the lake, this hotel can't be beaten for location. The languid nature of the lake, however, is reflected in the running of

the hotel and while the room rates are reasonable for the location, the rooms themselves are uninspiring – only the rooms with balconies overlooking the lake make this a good-value option.

🍴 Restaurants

Regional dishes, delicious seafood and great wines await, but make sure that the restaurant of your desires is open; opening times vary, although most open for lunch (1200-1500) and dinner (1900-2300) at least 6 days and nights a week. Keep in mind that most lakes restaurants close Dec-Jan, some staying shut as late as Mar, and some also close 1 night a week, generally a Mon or Tue.

Stresa p79

€€ Osteria degli Amici, Via Bolongaro 33, T0323-30453. This genial *osteria* is spread out over several rooms and has a tiny outdoor area where you can indulge in anything from a delicious pizza to a multiple course blow out. Menu highlights include risotto with porcini mushrooms or local fish.

€€ Piemontese, Via Mazzini 25, T0323-30235, www.ristorantepiemontese.com. This family-run restaurant is a local favourite, offering a choice between the elegant dining room or the vine-shaded courtyard. The cuisine consists of local classics presented with modern flair, and the service and wine list are the best in town.

€€ Ristorante del Pescatore, Vialo del Poncivo 3, T0323-31986. Renowned for its excellent seafood and while the grilled lake and ocean fish are excellent, they also do a Spanish paella, as well as fish stew – a tribute to the owners' Spanish origin. The seafood pastas are also a highlight of this petite restaurant.

Cafés
Most of Stresa's cafés and gelaterias are on and around the lake, such as **Pasticceria Jolly Bar** (via Principe Tomaso 17, Stresa), a big bustling place which also sells

scrumptious pastries and sweets, and **L'Idrovolante** (piazzale Lido 6, Stresa, T323-31384), a busy café-cum-bar-cum-restaurant on the water near the ferry dock that's popular for its superb coffee and pastries.

Verbania *p82*
Verbania is really divided into three areas: Pallanza, Suna and Intra, but most things of interest to visitors – diners especially – are in Pallanza, which is the area running along the waterfront and creeping up the hill behind. Due to the number of foreign visitors that invade Verbania each summer, you'll find a wide range of ethnic eateries, including Chinese, Indian, Japanese and Greek, most of which are mediocre and inauthentic. Unless you really need to satisfy a craving, it's best to stick to Italian fare.

€€€ Il Sole di Ranco, Piazza Venezia 5, Ranco, T0331-976507, www.ilsolediranco.it. Chef Davide Brovelli continues a family legacy at this restaurant with a summer and winter garden and an elegant interior. Expect premium ingredients to appear on the surprisingly lengthy menu, alongside creatively presented lake fish. With such an excellent wine cellar, it's probably a good idea to stay the night in one of the rooms upstairs.

€€ Da Cesare, Via Mazzini 14, Verbania, T0323-31386. From the hotel of the same name, this restaurant has a good reputation for dishes such as risotto with local fish, best taken on the outside terrace.

€€ Il Monastero, Via Castelfidardo 5/7, Suna, T0323-502544. This highly regarded restaurant has plenty of rustic elegance – not easy to achieve – and classic versions of local fish and meat dishes.

€€ Milano, Corso Zanitello 2, Pallanza, T0323-556816. A peaceful lakeside terrace is the setting for this local favourite. Not surprisingly the lake fish dishes are the hit of the menu, which also includes a fair share of classic regional specialities.

Cafés
There are myriad cafés and gelaterias on and around the waterfront in Pallanza but locals and tourists alike love **Gelateria Pasticceria Ciao Bella** (via San Vittore 61, T0323-519585).

Cannobio *p84*
€€ Lo Scalo, Piazza Vittoria Emanuele II 32, T0323-71480. The best expression of the cooking style of the region is to be found at this elegant restaurant, with excellent seafood (lake fish a speciality), painstaking presentation and a well-chosen wine list.

€€ Porto Vecchio, Piazza Vittorio Emanuele II, Cannobio, T0323-739639. The restaurant of the **Cannobio**, Porto Vecchio, is on a wonderful outdoor terrace that sets the scene for a romantic meal. The food (local specialities and Italian classics) is fine, as is the service and wine list.

Cafés
Cannobio has an array of alfresco cafés with tables overlooking the lake, and excellent gelaterie, conveniently located near the waterfront for when you're in the mood for a moonlit stroll with icecream in hand. For the best handmade gelato try **Gelateria Bar La Piazza** (piazza Vittorio Emanuele II 33, T0323-70496), **Gelatiere Di Zaccheo Dario** (via Magistris 63, T0323-71090) or **Bar Jolly Gelateria** (via Vittorio Emanuele II 24, T0323-71022), which also does good coffee.

Orta San Giulio *p85*
€€€ Villa Crespi, Via G Fava 18, Orta San Giulio, T0322-911902. If you need to rub your eyes in disbelief when you first sight the Moorish-themed Villa Crespi, the cuisine of chef Antonino Cannavacciuolo will have you repeating the gesture when each course of his perfectly crafted dishes arrive at the table. The skilful use of local ingredients and the balance of flavours sets a chef of this calibre well and truly apart from the rest.

€€ Osteria al Boeuc, Via Bersani 28, Novara, T0339-5840039. This ancient wine bar is worth visiting for the vino alone. They also do a selection of great cold cuts and snacks that perfectly compliment the local wines.

€€ Venus Ristorante, Piazza Motta 50, T0322-90362. It's hard to beat the summer terrace at this restaurant. Excellent local fare is on offer (and a good tasting menu), with a fine wine cellar and stellar desserts that will have you ordering that extra course.

Cafés

Arianna, Via Domodossola 10/12, Orta San Giulio Nordovest, T0332-911956. It may not be in the centre of the old village, but it's worth a trip for their delicious biscuits, the most famous of which is their Amaretti del Sacro Monte (moist almond biscuits).
Arte del Gelato, Via Olina 30, Orta San Giulio, T335-832 9298. Don't make a special trip, but if you are driving in or out of town, this superb gelateria in the modern centre, known as Orta San Giulio Nordovest, is worth a stop for their delicious artisanal gelato.
Leon d'Oro, Piazza Motta 43, Orta San Giulio, T0322-941991. Simple meals and snacks are served at this rather old-fashioned place on the main piazza. It won't win any gastronomic awards, and is much better for a coffee in the morning or an aperitivo in the evening. Pull up a chair at one of the floral covered tables under a shady umbrella and you can easily while away a couple of hours people-watching on the square.

Omegna

€ Salera 16, Piazza Salera 16, Omegna, T349-215 1632. A pleasingly modish café opposite the lake, it does great business with locals who drop in for its excellent coffee, substantial salads, fresh pastas and daily specials.

🌙 Bars and clubs

Maggiore and Orta aren't exactly the most happening lakes when it comes to entertainment, tending to attract more mature travellers or couples seeking romance. If you're after dance clubs, best head to the beaches or stay in Milan. However, no matter where you are on the lakes the thing to do in the late afternoon during the warmer months is to enjoy an aperitivo or two at a waterfront café-bar. Regardless of what you order, drinks often come with tiny complimentary dishes of snacks such as potato crisps, nuts, olives, cheese and salami cubes, and grissini. After dinner, head to the nearest gelateria for a gelato and a stroll along the lake's edge.

Lake Maggiore *p78*
Birreria Stregatto, Via Cadorna 20, Verbania. The courtyard here is the best place in town for a cold beer on a hot summer's day, and attracting mostly locals gives it a rare authenticity hard to find on this part of the lake.
Enoteca da Giannino, Via Garibaldi 32, Stresa. This busy little place might not be the most atmospheric of bars, but they have a good range of wines by the glass and fairly tasty snacks that do the trick.

Lake Orta *p85*
Caffè Jazz, Via Olina 13, Orta San Giulio, Lake Orta, T0322-911700. This cosy wine bar is the most atmospheric in Orta San Giulio, serving good wines by the glass to a cool jazz soundtrack.
Imbarcadero, Piazza Motta, Pella, Lake Orta, T0322-918003. Attracting everyone from local old fishermen for a beer to Milanese couples on holiday enjoying a quiet aperitivo, what makes this down-to-earth café-bar special is its tranquil waterfront location in one of the Lake Orta's most peaceful villages.

⊛ Festivals and concerts

Lake Maggiore *p78*
There are classical music concerts held frequently throughout the spring and summer months, from Mar-Sep, in towns, villages and islands around Lake Maggiore, under the umbrella of the **Stresa Festival**

(via Carducci 38, Stresa, T0323-31095, www.stresafestival.eu, €10-50). Venues range from atmospheric churches and villa gardens to town halls and waterfront promenades. Expect anything from Renaissance and baroque wind music to Mozart concertos, performed by everything from small ensembles to the Stresa Festival Orchestra to the Michael Nyman Band. See the website for programmes with full details.

On both Lake Maggiore and Lake Orta, café-bars are dotted around the waterfront and main squares. Most of the bars doubling as cafés open all day, from morning until fairly late at night, and might close 1 day a week, often Mon. Bars that mainly serve as wine bars tend to open around lunch and close after midnight.

Lake Orta p85
On Lake Orta, classical concerts are held as part of the Cusiano Festival of Antique Music in Jun, while jazz, blues, rock, folk and classical performances are held in a dozen towns and villages as part of the Il Lago della Musica series, from early Jun through to early Nov. Contact the tourist offices for details.

O Shopping

You'll find loads of little shops in Stresa, Verbania and Cannobio on Lake Maggiore and in Orta San Giulio on Lake Orta selling local crafts but, more often than not, very tacky souvenirs. Crafts include handmade and hand-painted ceramics, pottery and glassware. The best shopping on the lakes is found elsewhere, in Como and Bellagio; otherwise people simply head to Milan. Most shops open Mon-Sat 0930 or 1000, close for lunch at 1200 or 1300, then reopen 1600-1900. Those staying open on Sun during the busy summer tourist season may close one weekday (usually Mon) and open late another afternoon (often Tue).

Every day there are open-air markets on Maggiore and Orta lakes selling fresh fruit and vegetables, cheeses and cold cuts, flowers, clothes and other items. They are usually held on the main square and surrounding pedestrian streets and are easy enough to find. Mon: Baveno; Tue: Arona; Wed: Luino; Thu: Omegna; Fri: Stresa and Pallanza; Sat: Intra and Verbania; Sun: Cannobio.

Stresa p79
Food and drink
Pasticceria Gigi, Corso Italia 30, T0323-30225. In the business for 40 years, this bakery does tasty mini pizzas and pizza slices, which go down very nicely with a bottle of red.
Salumeria Musso di Bianchetti Augusto, Via Mazzini 1, T0323-30402. This shop boasts a great selection of cold cuts and fantastic regional salami.

Orta San Giulio p85
Art and antiques
The delightful village of Orta San Giulio is blessed with myriad shops selling antiques, collectables, and bric-a-brac on via Olina.

Food and drink
There's no shortage of atmospheric picnic spots at and around Orta San Giulio (from one of the benches under the shady trees on the main square to Isola di San Giulio itself) and there's no shortage of shops where you can stock your picnic basket.
Il Buongustaio, Piazza Ragazzoni, 8/10, Orta San Giulio, T0322-905626. A great one-stop-shop which boasts the best of the region including cheeses and cold cuts. The specialty is their salami, and there's a wide array to choose from, including salami of donkey, deer, wild boar, goat and goose, with truffles and with Barolo wine. Their wild boar bresaola and local mortadella are very good.
Panetteria Sappa, Piazza Motta 7, T0322-90416. Makes delicious fresh bread and focacce, tasty pizza slices, as well as pastries and cakes.

Souvenirs

Ricordi Orta San Giulio, Piazza Motta 30, Orta San Giulio, T0322-90337. This delightful shop has baskets out front overflowing with a huge array of fragrant handmade soaps, perfumes, essential oils and incense for the body and home, along with local crafts and souvenirs.

Silvia Rizzi, Piazza Motta 8, Orta San Giulio, T0322-90251. This young artisan uses traditional techniques to paint delicate fairies and maidens on porcelain. Not to everyone's taste but they make wonderful gifts for grandmothers and children, and her skills are impressive.

Vetroe' Di Berardi Stefania, Via Giovanetti 2/4, Orta San Giulio, T0322-905555. You'll find beautiful handmade glassware and other stunning glass objects, of both traditional and contemporary designs, for the home interior at this atelier of a local artist.

Omegna

Alessi, Via Privata Alessi 6, Crusinallo di Omegna, T0323-868648, www.alessi.com. Mon-Sat 0930-1800. This huge store adjoining the Alessi factory stocks the entire product range, the majority of which is at reduced outlet prices.

⏺ What to do

Lake Maggiore *p78*
Boating

Navigazione Lago Maggiore, Via F Baracca 1, Arona, T322-233200, www.navigazione laghi.it. The government-operated water transport for Lake Maggiore offers regular daily shuttle boats from Carciano (Stresa's lido) to Isola Bella and Isola Pescatori, as well as a range of cruises. These include excursions from Stresa or Laveno to Isola Bella, Isola Pescatori, and Isola Madre; tours to Switzerland, including a boat to Locarno; and the famous Lago Maggiore Express, a combined boat-train trip to Locarno Thu-Sun that trundles through stunning mountain and lake scenery. Mar-Sep only.

Food and drink

Il Gusto è a Monte, Tomassucci Travel Agency, piazza Marconi 3, Stresa, T323-933621, www.gustoamonte.it. This initiative by Verbano Ossola Province tourism offers 25 organized excursions, named 'Flavours of the Mountains', that provide a chance to taste and learn about local produce. Maggiore and Orta's gastronomic specialties include cured meats such as *violino di capra* (cured goat leg ham), alpine goat's cheeses like Bettelmatt, wild game including roe deer and boar, and Ossolano wine from Nebbiolo grapes. There are art, nature and architecture themed trips that incorporate walks to abandoned villages, ruined castles and lakes. If you speak Italian you can do a self-guided tour using a specially produced brochure to make your own arrangements to visit food producers of your choice.

Sports

Lago Maggiore Adventure Park, Strada Cavalli 18, Baveno, Stresa, T0323-919799, www.lagomaggioreadventurepark. com. Mar-Apr and Sep-Oct weekends and holidays 1000-1900, May-Jun daily 1000-1900, Jul-Aug 1000-2300, closed Nov-Feb. A fun adventure park offering a mountain bike range, climbing walls, junior and senior *percorso* (essentially tightrope walking), acrojumping (the opposite of bungy jumping), and an obstacle course with everything from monkey bars to upturned logs.

Monte Mottarone *p79*
Cable car

While Monte Mottarone, between Lake Maggiore and Lake Orta, is not the most impressive of mountains, if you're in the neighbourhood and dying to get your head in the clouds or are simply looking for a picnic spot with some altitude (1491 m) and Alpine and lake views, a cable car up the mountain for a picnic makes a fine excursion. Take the cable car (daily 0930-1730, every 20 mins, €12 return) from Carciano (on the shore opposite Isola

Bella) up to the summit. There is one stop at Alpino for Giardino Botanico Alpinia (at 804 m), which makes a pleasant diversion. Once at the top, picnic spots are easy to find; you can also rent bikes (around €25 a day).

Mountain climbing

Climbers can pick up a brochure (in English) from the tourist office called *Arrampicare al Mottarone*, produced by SnowFun Mottarone (www.mottaroneski.it) with diagrams detailing 9 different climbs, the degrees of difficulty, duration, and equipment needed. The climbing area is about a 30-min walk from the Mottarone summit and the brochure has directions for getting there. For more information see: www.arrampicando.it and www.cmvo.it, the website of the Comunita Montana Valle D'Ossola. The officially recommended Alpine climbing guide is Enzio Seppi (T322-900016).

Walking and trekking

If you're keen to do some walking or trekking in the mountains, pick up the brochure *Trekking alle pendici del Mottarone* (*Trekking the slopes of Mottarone*; Italian only but easy to follow) from the Stresa tourist office (via Canonica 8, T0323-31308). There are a handful of marked trails (some paved), ranging from easy walks on the lower slopes (including walks west to Belgirate at 260 m) to more strenuous treks up to the summit of Mottarone. All begin at Baveno, a suburb of Stresa just northeast of Carciano, and take 1½-5½ hrs.

If you want to do as the locals do, **Nordic walking** (involving more active use of the arms, like cross-country skiing) is the latest craze. The tourist office has a brochure *Trekking e Nordic Walking al Mottarone* (in English) with instructions on the walking technique and style, and several summit walks which leave from Bar Alp near the Mottarone summit; a 1-hr walk, Giro Rossa, takes you through the Cusio Valley for panoramic views of the Apennines to Monte Disgrazia.

Lake Orta *p85*
Boating

Isola di San Giulio, Piazza Motta Pier, Orta San Giulio, T333-605 0288. Motoscafi (small boats; €4.40 return, buy tickets from boat captain) depart every 15 mins for the 10-min ride across to Isola di San Giulio between 0900 and 1130 (breaking for lunch) and from 1300 to 1900. You can also opt for the **Giro Turistico** (tourist circuit; €8) which includes a return trip to the lake and town visit. While you'll notice tourists trying to bargain the price down, this is not a good way to make friends – the locals take great offence.

Walking and cycling

Ask at the Tourist Office of Orta San Giulio (see page 85) for a copy of the *Città di Orta San Giulio Map and Tourist Guide*, which includes a map and detailed directions for 5 return self-guided walks in and around Orta San Giulio, beginning from piazza Motta in the centre of Orta San Giulio: the 1st, and easiest, does a loop via the lakefront of the Orta San Giulio peninsula; the 2nd takes you through woods and fields via the hamlet of Carcegna to the waterfront village of Pettenasco; another follows a mule track to the villages of Vacciagheto and Miasino, while the last follows mule tracks to the hamlets of Vacciago and Lortallo, visiting 2 tiny frescoed churches and a Franciscan monastery with views of the lake and Monte Rosa.

Ecomuseo del Lago d'Orta e Mottarone, piazza Unita d'Italia 2, Pettenasco, T0323-89622. Pick up the brochure from the Ecomuseo del Lago d'Orta e Mottarone titled *Giro Lago*. The Giro Lago consists of over 500 km of itineraries you can do on bike and on foot, including 2 scenic circuits of the lake, offering vistas of Orta and other pre-Alpine lakes. The brochure has a map indicating which routes are asphalt and which are unpaved, and which parts are suited to walking or cycling.

Contents

Footprint features

Background

History

The northern Lombardy region of Italy, encompassing Milan and the glimmering Italian Lakes, has an action-packed history of battles, takeovers and power struggles. The region's geography has ruled its destiny and shaped its history. The Alps and Dolomites guard the northern, Germanic border and are believed to have formed each great glacial lake at the end of the last ice age. The longest Italian river, the Po, rushes through the region from the western Alps before emptying into the Adriatic, creating rich (and enviable) alluvial plains, valleys and fertile deltas along the way. Centrally located in Europe, and gateway to the Italian peninsula, the region's bounty and beauty have long attracted invaders and, when not consumed with in-fighting, the area has often found itself a pawn in power battles between foreign rulers.

Barbarian beginnings and Roman civilization

Visit the ancient rock art sites in Valcamonica, Brescia, and you'll be met with one of the world's richest collections of prehistoric petroglyphs – depictions of day-to-day life, warfare and belief – crafted by some of the earliest humans. Findings of arrows, axes and ceramics provide evidence that the region has been settled for millennia; artefacts and rock art show that a militaristic mindset was integral to the success of these early people.

Further south, and dating back to the seventh century BC, hardy Celtic peoples settled along the Po River (which, amazed by its scale, they called *bodincus* or 'bottomless') and held it – despite the growing might of the Latins and Etruscans who battled over central and southern Italy between the fifth and third centuries BC. There were periods of Etruscan rule (after they had spread from Tuscany) but these otherwise successful rulers ultimately fell to the Celtic tribes. The Celts began to create crude townships, which would in time become Milan, Como and the other towns and cities of the Lombardy region. The Po Valley's Celtic Boii clan were known as fierce fighters and their reputation largely protected them from attack. However, the Celtic tribes saw the success of the Latins and Etruscans in the south, and longed for expansion. Collectively named the Cisalpine Gaul ('Gaul on this side of the Alps') by the Latins, the trans-Alpine neighbours attempted a greed-driven attack on the Latin city of Rome. Unfortunately for the Celts, the fearful Roman forces had gathered an army to oppose them. Hopelessly disunited, the Celts gave battle until 233 BC and, with Milan as their last stronghold, the defeated tribes were ultimately driven back into the Alps.

The Romans triumphed in the north and became masters of the *Gallia Cisalpina* area, which is now Lombardy. Just as many regions asked themselves what the Romans had ever done for them, the answer in Lombardy was land-clearing, cultivation and roads – in short, modern civilization with advanced agriculture and trade. Under the Romans, Milan was called *Mediolanum*, which referred to its position in the 'middle of the plain', and its centrality meant that Milan became an important city along the trade route to Rome. By AD 300, Milan was considered the commercial capital of the western Roman Empire.

In AD 313 Emperor Constantine signed the Edict of Milan, which granted religious freedom, and Christianity became the state religion. People's favourite St Ambrose became a leading Christian ecclesiastical figure in the late fourth century, giving away his inherited lands and possessions before becoming bishop of Milan. He quelled religious factions and soothed Church-State tensions. He was known as the honey-tongued doctor because of his oratorical abilities; imagery related to bees and bee-keeping naturally followed, and this type of decoration can be spotted throughout Milan.

The factious tendencies of the local area and the wider empire, however, couldn't be overcome by one man. Constantine had united the Roman Empire's western and eastern (Byzantine) parts, but at the end of the fourth century it was divided again. There were constant raids from northern countries and, in AD 476, Rome and the western empire fell to the Teutonic invader Odovacer.

The Dark Ages

During the sixth century, Byzantium tried to wrest back control of the former western empire and the region's towns and cities became battlegrounds. A sort of peace was restored only after the invasion of the Po Valley by Germanic Lombards, who swept down from the north in AD 568 and subsequently ruled much of northern and central Italy for around 200 years. While some of the Lombards were, at least initially, pagan, others were Christian and they built many churches – often over sites of pagan worship.

In the eighth century the Germanic Franks seized a proportion of Lombard territory – and granted a sizeable proportion of the land to the Pope, thus strengthening papal power. In AD 774 the Frankish king and militant Christian, Charlemagne conquered the Lombards and when northern Italy was safely in his grasp, he moved on to seize a vast swathe of southern Italy. In AD 800 he had the Pope crown him Holy Roman Emperor, a title that made him the assumed heir to the original western Roman Empire. Charlemagne was known as the 'father of Europe' until his death in AD 814. The wealth and power of the Church was evident in the extravagance of the buildings and monuments, and the Christian social structures that survived beyond Charlemagne's life.

The development of Lombardy now unravels into a bewildering tangle of historical threads. After Charlemagne's death, the major cities began to operate as independent, self-governing states, each ruled by a commune. This was an association of the great and the good (well, the rich and powerful) and generally included merchants and lawyers. The city state began to rise, able to shrug off traditional land-owning rural systems in favour of commerce, finance and banking. The enterprising class of the communes extended their activities into the rest of Europe: so much so that 'Lombard' is still a known term for bankers and money-changers.

The city states soon began to jostle for power and as they became increasingly wealthy, so each began to cast an acquisitive eye on its neighbour. The situation was already complicated enough – but now a religious element fired the cities' competitive fervour. Relations between the papacy and the empire had been strained for some time when a new Teutonic aggressor, Frederick I of the Hohenstaufen dynasty, marched into Italy and seized as much of the northern and central lands as he could. Frederick, nicknamed Barbarossa ('red beard'), had himself crowned King of Italy and Holy Roman Emperor. He also appointed an imperial official, a *podestà*, to each commune to help wield his power.

Many communes resented this display of force, but the northern region took it particularly badly and banded together against Barbarossa. The Lombard League had the support of the Pope, who wished to see less imperial rule in Italy. The League fought under one flag, the Milanese red cross, hoisted from a *carroccio* – an oxen-driven war cart that served to rally the formerly disparate groups. After a Lombard victory at Legnano in 1176, Barbarossa's family and supporters – thinking he was dead – began mourning their leader. He arrived home some days later, battered and red-faced. Unable to defeat the Lombard League, he signed a tentative peace agreement with the Pope.

Further conflict ensued later when Barbarossa's son and successor Henry VI died, and his child Frederick II was considered too young for the imperial role. Henry's brother, Philip, laid claim to the title of Holy Roman Emperor instead. His claim was heartily disputed by Otto of Brunswick and the Pope determinedly supported his claim. Frederick II eventually became Holy Roman Emperor in 1220, and fought against Otto for control of much of Italy. The death of Frederick II in 1250 was a turning point for the political health of the region's communes, as his threatened intervention in the politics of the north had kept the communes of the Lombard League united against a common foe. Faced once more with a power vacuum, the medieval communes fell to the rise of dynastic rule. When the new middle class of successful merchants grew in power, they ultimately developed political clout and the result was a tendency of one supreme family to effectively govern a city. This political system, called *signoria*, replaced the communes.

The Renaissance

Throughout Europe, the ways of the medieval 'dark ages' were eschewed, replaced by a brighter, enlightened era that focused on a finer appreciation of the arts and literature. Disunity between the northern city-states and their ruling *signori* spurred creative, rather than military, competition. This initiated an exciting period of prolific artistic production, the commissioning of extravagant state buildings, and the creation of wealth for individuals as well as for states. The spirit of individuality and creativity that developed during this period is still very much a part of the northern Italian psyche today.

Understandably, the *signoria* system had many flaws. There were ensuing rivalries between families, expansionist and defensive strategies, as well as familial conflicts. One such family was the Visconti dynasty of Milan, who succeeded in wresting control of the city from the ruling della Torre family, taking residence in the Palazzo Reale. Much of the Visconti dynasty's success came from Gian Galeazzo Visconti who, upon becoming Duke of Milan in 1395, greatly increased the family's expansionist efforts. Gian Galeazzo commenced work on a vast castle in Milan (which would later be named the Castello Sforzesco, after the next dynasty to reside there) and commissioned the building of the Gothic-themed Duomo, the heart of Milan even to this day. Galeazzo died in 1402, by which time much of the northern Italian regions were under Milanese rule. In his absence, however, the Visconti family's dominance diminished and had virtually vanished by the mid-15th century. The Visconti name, though, still commands extraordinary respect to this day.

For the next three years the Ambrosian Republic, named after the earlier St Ambrose, was relatively peacefully self-ruled and battles, temporarily, became a thing of the past. But by 1450, another dynasty began to take shape, led by Francesco Sforza, who played a great part in enhancing the region's artistic wealth. He was a generous patron and under Sforza's benevolent rule Milan prospered. Work was restarted on the Visconti Castle, now renamed Castello Sforzesco, by which it is still known today.

Francesco's successor Lodovico Sforza was an even greater patron of the arts, and his support for creative endeavour resulted in what came to be known as the region's golden age. But it was not only art and architecture that benefited. Agriculture in the rich soil of the Po Plain developed through irrigation initiatives led by the ubiquitous Leonardo da Vinci – who also started to paint *The Last Supper* around this time. Rice cultivation, cheese and butter production all flourished, and continue to distinguish northern cuisine well into the 21st century.

The Italian Wars and foreign occupation

The growing wealth of the region inevitably attracted foreign interest and when organized French armies defeated an unprepared and complacent Italian army at the Battle of Fornovo in 1495 and invaded the northern Lombardy region, they broke the Italian spirit for the next 300 years.

Thus followed the period dubbed The Italian Wars, during which the north was invaded first by the French, then by the Spanish, and finally by the Austrians. The Sforza dynasty's rule of Milan collapsed entirely in 1499, and the Italians' will to fight seemed at it lowest. The pressured circumstances brought on by occupation led to the Milanese government changing 11 times during the first 30 years of the 16th century.

The French army was eventually defeated by Spanish forces in the Battle of Pavia in 1525, and in the Treaty of Cambrai in 1529 French rule was ceded to Spain, with King Charles V crowned King of Italy. Fierce battles between the French, Spanish and Lombards continued, with France ultimately relinquishing the much-prized Lombardy region to Spain, which then governed the area for the next two centuries.

By the mid-17th century, the years of foreign occupation were beginning to take their toll on this once prosperous region. Lombardy was hit by economic recession mainly caused by the disruption to agriculture and textile production brought on by years of war. Plague then followed – described in Alessandro Manzoni's hugely influential book *I Promessi Sposi* (The Betrothed) – which devastated the region's crop production, leading to a decline in the population.

By the 18th century, however, shifts in the balance of power in western Europe began to take place, with a positive impact on Lombardy. The Treaty of Aix-la-Chapelle of 1748 left Austria in charge of the region, in place of the Spanish. The Austrians had a stabilizing effect, with the more progressive Habsburg dynasty heralding the the beginning of The Enlightenment. Debate began about the need for reform, with intellectuals such as Pietro Verri and Cesare Beccaria in Milan joining discussions with intellectuals from other parts of Italy and around Europe about the causes of underdevelopment in Italian states in comparison to the rest of Europe.

The Roman Catholic Church was identifiedas the most significant obstacle to progress, and radical economic and social reforms led to the development of a counter-clerical movement. By the 1790s the Church had lost much of its power, particularly in the Lombardy region. At the same time the impact of the French Revolution was felt particularly strongly in a country undergoing its own radical reforms, leaving Italy more susceptible to the tumultuous changes sweeping Europe.

The Risorgimento

When Napoleon invaded Italy in 1796, the people rose up against the ruling Austrians, forming several French-run republics, which were ultimately overthrown. The many Franco-Austrian battles of the French Revolution in northern Italy paved the way for the Italian revolt against foreign occupation and, finally, the emergence of a united Italy. During Napoleon's reign, France repeatedly occupied, and lost to Austria, the Lombardy region. Following his defeat in Russia in 1814, Napoleon abdicated and, in the same year, the Congress of Vienna made Austria the dominant power in Italy. This period is seen as a turning point in Italian political reform and the start of the Risorgimento – or 'Revival'.

Grand Touring the grand lakes

The lakes of the north of Italy have been noted for their beauty since ancient Roman times and have always been a place of retreat and reflection. But it wasn't until the notion of the Grand Tour that writing about the lakes made them popular with these new travellers from England, other parts of Europe and America. These privileged travellers were also intrepid, for in the 18th century one could not know whether they would be attacked by bandits and robbed, or perhaps stuck for weeks due to bad weather. But by the mid-1800s, guidebooks began to appear, such as the brown-clothed *Murrays* in 1842, which described several itineraries for the Lombardy region, with visits to Villa Carlotta, Villa d'Este and Villa Serbelloni.

The route over the Simplon to the Lakes was a rite of passage for Grand Tourists and by this time was in good enough shape, thanks to Napoleon, to be tackled by these travellers with their comfortable carriages. Lake Como, in particular, had become an artists' retreat and writers and musicians – themselves some of the first Grand Tourists – flocked to the lake for inspiration. By the time American novelist Edith Wharton's *Italian Villas and Their Gardens* was published in 1904, the secret of the beauty of the lakes had reached beyond the Grand Tourists. But the lakes have never shaken the romance of those days when author Henry James wrote to his sister, 'one can't describe the beauty of the Italian lakes, nor would one try if one could…'.

Austria held a particularly fierce grip on the Lombardy region, one characterized by a large agricultural population, a declining and impoverished middle class, and a handful of intellectuals with revolutionary ideals for a unified Italy. Unrest spread throughout the region, making an uprising against the Austrians inevitable. The first occurred in 1820, following the Austrian repression of the pro-unity Lombardy publication *Il Conciliatore* (The Peacemaker) and the imprisonment of its publishers and writers.

As a result of Austria's reactionary control, nationalist unification ideas gained popularity. All the while, more and more radical ideas filtered through from a rapidly changing Europe, culminating in the continent-wide revolution of 1848. In Italy the First War of Italian Independence was fought on many fronts, initially in Sicily, then in Tuscany where constitutions were granted, and also in Milan where the *Cinque Giornate* (Five Days) revolt forced the Austrians out of the city during a siege which ended with a provisional government being set up. Just three months later the Austrians, led by septuagenarian Field Marshal Radetzky, returned and reclaimed Milan and nearby Brescia (which was nicknamed 'The Lioness' following its brave fighting during a 10-day anti-Austrian uprising).

The unification movement was not to be repressed for long. Several leading personalities emerged and gathered support from all classes across Italy's regions. Giuseppe Mazzini was an early leader in the Risorgimento movement, later exiled to England from where he orchestrated many revolts under the *Giovane Italia* (Young Italy) organization – a group dedicated to resisting Austrian rule. In 1848 nationalists Camillo Benso di Cavour and Cesare Balbo together pursued a constitution and wrote and published the *Statuto* (Statute), which was to eventually become the basis of the constitution of the Kingdom of Italy in 1861. It was the charismatic Giuseppe Garibaldi, though, who proved to be the most popular hero of the unification movement, garnering huge support up and down the country.

Cavour was elected prime minister of the Piedmont kingdom, securing the support of its armed forces and, gradually, of the French army under Napoleon III. Together the armies gathered to fight Austria in Lombardy in the Second War of Italian Independence in 1859. The combined forces defeated the Austrians in battles at Magenta and Solferino, and Lombardy was ceded to the Piedmontese. However, a quick peace treaty signed between the weary French and Austrians undid all the hard work, and Lombardy was once again in Austrian hands – this time as an Italian Republic. The fight for unification was on once more, with Cavour leading the way this time.

By 1861 Cavour had succeeded in bringing Milan and the Lombard states into the newly formed Kingdom of Italy. Italy was now unified under Piedometese leadership, with Cavour and Balbo's historic *Statuto* of 1848 forming the basis of a new constitution which established the three classic branches of government: the executive (the king); the legislative; and the judiciary (appointed by the king).

Fascism and the World Wars

The new Kingdom of Italy faced many challenges as agricultural production was in decline and farmers were increasingly impoverished. The textile industry, however, was growing, leading to the relatively fast return of Milan and the Lombard states to their former wealth. The southern states of Italy remained poor, with many southerners migrating north (and overseas) to pursue a better life.

The newly united Italy was under pressure to secure strategic foreign alliances and in 1882 an agreement was signed by the monarchy to secure a largely secret Triple Alliance with Germany and Austria-Hungary. The people's old ally France was notably excluded.

The monarchy set about enlarging the nation's armed forces, and military spending increased by 40%.

In Milan, splendid new state works commenced under Vittorio Emanuele II including the piazza del Duomo and Galleria Vittorio Emanuele II, railways were extended to link Milan with its northern industrial neighbours of Turin and Genoa, electric lighting was installed in the La Scala opera house, and in 1875 a free newspaper, *Corriere della Sera* (Evening Courier) was published for the masses.

In Milan and Turin major new industries grew, and by 1899 car production plants had been established. Such rapid industrialization led to the organization of factory workers into trade unions, leading in turn to the development of socialist ideas. In 1898 unrest amongst workers began to erupt and major protests occurred over the high price of bread. Reaction was swift and brutal and hundreds were killed in Milan when General Bava Beccaris opened fire on protesting crowds in the piazza del Duomo. One standout socialist who began to emerge in Milan in the early 1900s was the young Benito Mussolini, editor of socialist newspaper *Avanti!* (Forward!).

By 1910, a growing opposition force called the Nationalist Association had formed, comprised of those conservatives and imperialists who supported the Triple Alliance, the protectionist foreign policy, and strict state control of labour and production. By 1914, when the Great War broke out in neighbouring Austria-Hungary, Italy was in a state of flux, as few of its population would support a war in alliance with Austria against France.

Italy remained indecisively neutral until August 1915. The large body of socialists were content to stay out of the war, but a smaller group of nationalist interventionists, along with the militant Futurists (see page 104), were wealthier, more combative, and more passionate about Italy's place in the war. During this period, Mussolini resigned from his role at *Avanti!* and took up with the interventionists at *Popolo d'Italia* (People of Italy), the media vehicle for leading the masses to war and later the foundation for the Fascist movement. Italy would enter the First World War a divided and ill-prepared nation, fighting on two fronts, at home and away. Italy had fought alongside the Allies and expected just rewards from the Treaty of Versailles, but instead was at best overlooked and at worst humiliated. Italy had fought a very costly war and was left with high inflation and unemployment, the perfect ingredients for an emerging nationalist leader.

Following the First World War, Mussolini formed the nationalist Fascist Party in 1919, holding party meetings at Palazzo Castini in Milan. Its rise in popularity coincided with the rise of post-war trade unions formed by starving workers. In 1922, Mussolini came to power after the Fascist March on Rome, and the intimidated Vittorio Emanuele III handed him the reins of government. By 1924, Mussolini, now Prime Minister, was calling himself *Il Duce* (the Leader).

From the mid-1930s the Fascists, now clearly an expansionist party, invaded Libya and neighbouring Abyssinia (present-day Ethiopia). International protests were loud, with the exception of Hitler's Germany. The two leaders held similar beliefs and in 1939 signed the Pact of Steel, securing an alliance between Germany and Italy. When Hitler invaded Poland later in the year, Italy remained outwardly neutral, but as Germany's victories added up, Mussolini wanted a piece of the action and, in 1940, looked to Greece for his wartime coup. Italy suffered terrible losses, however, and Germany had to intervene to avoid a certain Italian defeat.

By the summer of 1943, it was clear that Italy, and, in turn, Mussolini's Fascist regime, were in deep trouble. When Mussolini was ousted, his standing was such that barely a protest was heard and, after a period of unrest, Italy declared war against its former ally, Germany. Initially arrested but later freed, Mussolini went to face Hitler, who sent him back to Italy to set up the Italian Social Republic, which he established at German-controlled Salò on 23 September, 1943. This fragile puppet government was always in a tenuous situation, with the Allies taking more and more of Italy's territory, but it served Hitler well as a way of repressing the partisans fighting against the Germans in northern Italy. As the end of the war inevitably drew near, on 25 April, 1945, the Italian Social Republic disintegrated, with Mussolini and his mistress caught fleeing Italy. They were executed on Lake Como on 28 April, 1945.

The Italian Republic

The years immediately following the Second World War were difficult for Italy, which was forced to pay reparations. The country's economy was once again weak and fragmented and in 1946 a referendum saw the monarchy defeated. Italy officially became a republic and a new constitution came into effect on 1 January 1948.

In 1957, Italy became a founding member of the European Economic Community thus becoming part of a broader Europe – a positive step forward for both the nation's morale and economy. The north entered a period of industrialization, based on a new infrastructure funded by the USA under the Marshall Plan, and burgeoining industries in chemicals, iron, steel and cars helped to finally set the economy on track.

Milan continued to form one corner of the industrial triangle with neighbours Turin and Genoa. Large exhibition centres were constructed in the north to support trade and industry, and in 1965 the Mont Blanc tunnel opened, thus paving the way for tourism to flourish. The economic success of the industrial north, however, overshadowed the importance of agriculture, and once again poor southerners migrated north to find work and economic prosperity.

By the end of the 1960s, the economic boom was over and political and industrial unrest began to appear, marked first by the student protests of 1968. There followed a period of anti-state terrorism by right- and left-wing extremist groups, the first instance of which was an explosion in a bank on piazza Fontana in Milan's city centre, killing hundreds. A neo-fascist terrorist movement called *Brigate Rosse* (Red Brigade) grew to prominence during the 1970s, formed from within the factories and universities of Milan and the other towns and cities of Lombardy. The Red Brigade would be held responsible for the assassination of former Prime Minister Aldo Moro in 1978, for which 32 Brigade members were imprisoned.

The 1980s and 1990s were marked by political scandals that rocked Italy, revealing extensive corruption in Milan, referred to as *Tangentopoli* (Bribesville). The national *mani pulite* (clean hands) investigation uncovered Milan's rotten core in 1992, sparking betrayals, despair, and suicides by some of the accused, marking the end of the First Republic and many of the political parties that had dominated the political landscape since the end of the Second World War. Mario Chiesa of the supposedly squeaky-clean Italian Socialist Party was the first to be arrested and tried. He had been quickly condemned by party leader Bettino Craxi who called him a *mariuolo* or 'villain', though Craxi himself was arrested a short time later. Betrayals led to a string of arrests in Milan and the north across the whole political spectrum and within industry and commerce.

In the political power vacuum that followed such widespread and devastating political change, the far-right Lega Nord (Northern League) rose to power.

Organized crime continued its fearsome grip on Milan and welfare reforms were put in place in the 1990s to try to control this destabilizing situation. Wealthy Milanese businessman Silvio Berlusconi came to power in 1994 under the right-wing *Polo per la Libertà* (Freedom Alliance) and despite tumultuous times in the 1990s and 2000s – for a while, the average length of government was just 11 months – remained the one constant figure in Italian politics until the markets lost confidence in him in late 2011. Mario Monti took over but tendered his resignation just over a year later. At the time of writing, Berlusconi had announced he was running again for election, due to be held at the end of February 2013.

Art and architecture

Medieval, Romanesque and Gothic

Milan and the smaller towns dotted around the Lombardy and lakes neighbourhood, such as Como and Brescia, offer a marvellous sample of the country's superb art and architecture from the medieval, Romanesque and Gothic movements, which span a period beginning around AD 400 and lasting until the 14th century. Lombardy was well heeled during the Middle Ages and the mighty Catholic Church invested extravagant sums to construct spectacular monuments that sometimes took centuries to finish. Fortunately, many of those have survived to this day.

Art

The best place in the region to see art from the Middle Ages is at the **Museo d'Arte Antica** (Museum of Ancient Art) at Milan's **Castello Sforzesco** (see page 30), although the castle's Pinacoteca (art gallery) and the **Pinacoteca di Brera** (see page 36), all boast art from the medieval period. The Museo d'Arte Antica hosts room after room of mosaics, sculptures, frescoes and even remnants of the city's architecture. There is an impressive display of Lombard (as well as Roman and Byzantine) sculptures from the Early Christian period through the early Middle Ages. Works include the *Testa di Teodora* (Head of Theodora, the Byzantine Empress), a stunning sixth century marble sculpture, along with beautiful decorative floor mosaics and marble reliefs from Milan's ancient churches of Santa Tecla, San Protaso ai Monaci and Santa Maria d'Aurona.

Among the frescoes and sculptures on display at the museum from the Romanesque and Gothic periods are architectural pieces such as capitals and shelves crafted by local artisans. These have been found in churches in Milan and Pavia and feature intricate carvings of mermaids, dragons, lions and other beasts, real and mythical. There are also some fine examples of Romanesque sculpture and carved capitals from Como and Cremona.

Architecture

It may be the major city of the region, with a long, action-packed history, but apart from its monumental **Duomo** (see page 20), Milan's architectural delights are often overlooked by travellers, despite the city boasting some of the most impressive examples of medieval architecture in northern Italy. Piazza Mercanti, for instance, is an atmospheric marketplace that first took shape in 1228. Elsewhere, the Archi di Porta Nova is the only remaining part of the city's medieval walls and is adorned with sculptures of the Madonna and Child.

The **Basilica di Sant'Ambrogio** (see page 43) was built in honour of Milan's first bishop, St Ambrose. Considered to be a significant and fine example of Lombard Romanesque architecture, it became a model for many of the region's basilicas. It boasts a beautiful colonnaded quadrangle with columns carved with strange beasts, and a pulpit also adorned with wild animals. The building features Germanic influences that are the result of centuries of combative contact between the Lombards and neighbouring Germanic kingdoms. Artistic and architectural influences from the two groups during this period are so intertwined that it's difficult for all but avid architectural buffs to distinguish the features that identify their true origins.

The web-like layout of Milan has as its heart the colossal Duomo, the world's largest Gothic cathedral and Europe's second biggest cathedral after St Peter's in Rome. Started in 1386, it was constructed from rare Candoglia marble and boasts 135 spires, some 150 stained glass windows, countless intricate carvings and imposing buttresses, and a mind-boggling 3,400 statues. Leonardo da Vinci was integral to the cathedral's construction, creating a canal lock system which allowed the enormous stone slabs to be brought to the site. The gilded *Madonnina* (Little Madonna) sitting atop the Duomo's highest steeple is there to protect the city spread out before her.

Renaissance

When travellers think of Italian art they inevitably think of works from the Renaissance period. The Renaissance, or 're-birth' (*Rinascimento* in Italian), heralded a revolutionary movement away from the dark Middle Ages and towards a vibrant period of creative endeavour that saw the flourishing of art, architecture, literature and music.

Whilst much of the Renaissance action was centred on Florence and Venice, the movement quickly travelled to Milan and the wealthier northern regions, and later to Germany and northern Europe where it became known as the Northern Renaissance. One explanation for the impetus of the Italian Renaissance is the long-running series of wars and the intense rivalry between Milan and Florence, which had motivated Gian Galeazzo Visconti (Milan's ruler 1378-1402) to build a great empire in northern Italy.

When Francesco Sforza came to power in Milan in 1447 with similar ambitions to Visconti, he quickly transformed medieval Milan into an important centre for the arts, culture and learning. Sforza may have been ruthless but he was a generous patron and benevolent ruler. Sforza supported Renaissance greats such as as Leonardo da Vinci, the Milanese painters Ambrogio Bergognone, Andrea Solari and Vincenzo Foppa, and the Lombard architects Giovanni Antonio Amadeo and Donato Bramante. As a result Milan now boasts some of the finest works of Italian Renaissance art and architecture.

Art

The art from this period in particular is now considered to be among some of the world's greatest, including Leonardo da Vinci's *Mona Lisa* (on display at The Louvre in Paris) and *Il Cenacolo* (The Last Supper, see page 34), both of which draw an astonishing number of visitors each day. Housed in the refectory of Milan's **Santa Maria delle Grazie** (see page 34), the painstakingly restored mural of *Il Cenacolo* is so precious it can only be viewed by small groups for a limited time. The Museo d'Arte Antica at Castello Sforzesco contains more da Vinci frescoes in the Sala delle Asse, along with Michelangelo's unfinished work, *Rondanini Pietà*, which he was working on when he died in 1564.

The **Pinacoteca Ambrosiana** (see page 23) is found within what was Europe's first public library and is home to Italy's first still life, Carravaggio's *Canestro di Frutta* (Basket of Fruit) and da Vinci's *Musico* (Musician), as well as works by Tiepolo, Titian and Raphael. The **Museo Poldi Pezzoli** (see page 27) is another great source of Renaissance treasures including the *Madonna della Loggia* (Mother and Child) by the Florentine School's master Botticelli.

Architecture

Notable architecture from the Renaissance includes Milan's striking red-brick **Castello Sforzesco**, which had been the Visconti castle. Leonardo da Vinci was a consulting engineer at the Sforza court and was responsible for some of its renovations, designing some of the castle's defence mechanisms, as well as the Navigli (the city's waterways). Another wonderful example of architecture from the period is the splendid Renaissance courtyard which united the city's hospitals into the great Ospedale Maggiore, better known these days as Ca' Granda. It was designed by Tuscan architect Filarete and encompassed work by Solari, Amadeo and Richini.

20th century

Futurism and Fascism

At the end of the 19th century the late-starting Italy experienced the Second Industrial Revolution, and the prevailing social and economic conditions by the start of the 20th century ensured the timing was right for the birth of the Futurist movement (see page 99).

The founder of the Italian movement, writer Filippo Tommaso Marinetti, launched the *Manifesto del Futurismo* on 20 February 1909, in which he expressed a hatred of tradition, writing: "We want no part of it, the past, we the young and strong Futurists!" Instead, they desired a modern industrial city, technology over nature, urban living over country life, and preferred speed to the slower pace of the past.

The Futurist members were anarchists, nationalists and socialists initially, and while young socialist-nationalist leader Benito Mussolini had no personal interest in art, he supported their movement while funding a number of projects by artists and architects in order to buy their loyalty.

When the First World War came to an end, Mussolini announced his rather Futurist-inspired intention to speed up the reconstruction of Italy and dedicated funds to developing the railways and other public works. Initiated as far back as 1906 by Vittorio Emanuele III, the monumental **Stazione Centrale** was completed in 1931. The railway station's initial design by Milan-based architect Ulisse Stacchini had been simple, but under Mussolini's orders, it became increasingly grand as he wanted it to be a symbol of Fascist power. It's now recognized as one of the world's finest railway stations.

Under state patronage, art and architecture thrived during the period between the World Wars. A modern Rationalist-influenced architectural movement was born, pioneered largely by Giuseppe Terragni, a Milan-based architect who worked under Mussolini's regime. Terragni's most famous building was the innovative, contemporary-looking Casa del Fascio at Como, started in 1932 and finished in 1936, which was originally intended to function as a striking backdrop for mass Fascist rallies. During this period a series of art shows were launched, including **La Triennale** (see page 34) in Milan.

Brutalist Modernism

After the Second World War destroyed many of Milan's buildings, reconstruction and functionality took priority over form and style, and the practicalities of rebuilding shaped the architectural themes of the time. By 1950, a new architectural movement was born – Brutalist Modernism. The architects Banfi, Belgiojoso, Peressutti and Rogers, who became known as BBPR, designed the revolutionary **Torre Velasca**, completed in 1957. As space was at a premium in modern Milan, its base was built narrower than the rest of the building while protruding buttresses supported the upper, wider storeys. A modern interpretation of a medieval castle, the 20-storey tower draws on the medieval and Gothic architectural themes that are so much a part of Milan's makeup, such as the Duomo and the Castello Sforzesco.

Design in Milan and Lakes Como and Maggiore

Celebrated as a global design capital, Milan is a city where designers are nurtured and revered. The home of cutting edge fashion, furniture, lighting, interior, and product designers, the world's eyes are always on the region to see what will be produced and where future trends lie.

Milan and its surrounding provinces have been synonymous with great design for almost a century. Italians like to say that the region was built on the back of design, with so many sectors of the economy from Milan to Como contributing to, and flourishing from, the ever-evolving design industry. A region of unsurpassed imagination, innovative and intense creativity, its success is due to the fact that it has the industrial and manufacturing infrastructure to make radical ideas a reality.

Milan's world-famous design shows and fairs were founded in the early 20th century to showcase the most inspiring selection of designs and inventions. A selection of the region's most fêted works are on show at **La Triennale** (see page 34), Milan's main design museum. A turning point for design in the lakes was the end of the Second World War, after which followed a period that produced a new wave of Italian designers as the country was physically (and morally) rebuilt. Notably, Corradino released the Vespa scooter in 1946, which became the main form of transport for Italians. The Vespa was an ideal, affordable means of negotiating the congested streets and the mobility it provided revolutionized Italian society. The scooter's enduring design is a worldwide symbol of Italian youth, freedom and effortless chic.

During the 1960s and 1970s Italian designers experimented with plastics, glass and other materials in the Radical Design period, always with functionality and space as the springboard for their innovation. Carlo Bugatti designed his famous chairs, Joe Colombo released the *Tube Chair*, and Guzzini acrylic homeware took the world by storm.

The 1980s saw the Lake Orta-based Alessi plastic kitchenware brand emerge and grow as Alessi recruited different designers to work with the company, leading it to cult celebrity status with its fun and colourful range – most famously Philippe Starck's *Juicy Salif* three-legged juicer and Michael Graves' whistling bird kettle.

The 1990s saw Milanese plastic furniture designer Kartell gain a dedicated following – Ron Arad's curved *Bookworm Bookshelf* was its breakthrough release – and the company became famous for its chic transparent chairs. A string of prominent architects and interior designers incorporated Kartell's sleek Poliform furniture into projects, catapulting the company to global cool status by the end of the century.

Another towering landmark from the 1950s is the **Pirelli Tower**, built in 1950. Designed by architect Giò Ponti, it was commissioned by Alberto Pirelli, director of the famous tyre company, to be built on the site of his tyre factory which had been bombed during the Second World War. Admired for its lofty proportions and design elegance, it remains a symbol of the economic prosperity of Milan and northern Italy.

Nature and environment

The Italian Lakes boast sparkling expanses of water variously surrounded by softly undulating hills, serrated limestone cliffs, lofty mountains and lush agricultural plains, with the ever-present snow-clad Alps providing a dramatic backdrop. Dotted across Lombardy and straddling the borders with Piedmont and the Veneto, the lakes are where the northern Italians go to play, especially the Milanese and Veronese.

Alpine glaciers formed the glistening lakes of Como, Maggiore, Garda, Iseo, Orta and the others. Spanning 600 km from east to west and separating Italy from its northern neighbours, France and Switzerland (and further east Austria and Slovenia), the icy Alps are nearly always alluringly visible from the lakes. The Italian Alps provide a winter wonderland to escape to for skiing and snow sports during the cold months while their emerald slopes, blanketed in forest with limestone peaks poking through the clouds, provide ideal conditions for hiking, Nordic walking and climbing in the summertime.

The lakes may be lovely but they are also located in Italy's most highly populated and industrialized region. Travellers often forget that this complex natural landscape is home to scores of cities, hundreds of towns, and thousands of villages and hamlets, and the industry that has made the region so wealthy and given it such an outstanding quality of life is spread throughout. An agriculturally rich region, it has emerged as a major supplier of food to the rest of Italy, as well as establishing itself as a key exporter to the rest of the world.

So while there are plenty of opportunities to get out and enjoy the area's natural environment, unfortunately the air is not always as fresh as it could be and poor water quality occasionally means swimming in some of the lakes is not always advisable.

Heading for the hills
For those of you who want to experience nature in winter but don't want to fasten on skis, snow-shoeing is popular, while in summer the best way to experience the environment is to head for the hills, which in the warmer months are alive with hikers and Nordic walkers (more invigorating than your average stroll) enjoying the vibrant wildflowers that blanket the mountain meadows. All of the tourist offices in the region have information on organized hikes and hiring private guides or, at the very least, can provide good maps and itineraries for self-guided walks on sign-posted trails.

The area has dedicated areas to protect flora and fauna, including national parks, which are never more than a couple of hours' drive away. Northern Italy boasts dozens of national parks, the most popular and most accessible to Milan and the lakes being the Parco Nazionale del Gran Paradiso (Grand Paradise National Park) and Parco Nazionale della Val Grande (Great Valley National Park) in Piedmont. For details of a drive round the Great Valley National Park, see page 84.

Rivers, mountains, marshes and markets
The Po Basin, which makes up the rough boundaries of the northern Lombardy region, dictates the nature of this remarkable landscape. The basin, at the foot of the mountains to the north, and Italy's longest river, the Po (645 km) to the south, is filled with silt from the mountains, forming the plain. The plain is less fertile in the far north and richer the closer it gets to the river, and industry and agriculture have developed accordingly.

The main forested areas of the region are at the base of the mountains, where oak, olive and cypress trees thrive, while higher up the alpine flanks beech trees flourish, along with spruce and juniper. This is the main habitat of wildlife in this densely populated northern region, which is home to ibex and deer, and the rare brown bear. Alpine birds, including black grouse and the golden eagle, are spotted here.

The swampy marshland was considered ideal for rice production, so is home to rice paddies that produce one third of Italy's rice for risotto and other short grain rice dishes. Some of Italy's most prized risotto rice comes from the paddies surrounding Mantua in the region's east. Grapes are also grown in the region – where aren't they in Italy? – and the cool climate reds grown on the steep slopes of the Valtellina area are particularly delicious. Valtellina is the 'green' area along the north of Lombardy running along the foot of the Alps on the Swiss border. Agriculturally rich, fresh food markets are held in the market square of most towns and villages and there are annual produce festivals to herald rice, asparagus, wine and white truffle harvests. It's a pretty area, popular for skiing, cycling, hiking, and spa treatments in the thermal springs.

Milan's bowl v nature's fruit bowl

At around 120 m above sea level, and roughly halfway between the arid northern and swampy southern sections of the plain, Milan sits in the centre of the Po Basin with hills and mountains all around. The city's environment is marked by the pollution that accompanies any industrial city but the problem is compounded in Milan by the city's climate (characterised by damp, cold winters with occasional snow from December to February, and hot humid summers with temperatures rising to 30°C in summer) and bowl-like geography that means the pollution can't escape. This means Milan is sometimes covered in a light smog or fog, creating stunning photo opportunities when only the church spires are visible. Milan's residents cope by getting away to the lakes when it becomes too much!

The smaller towns and cities in the region each have very different environments and landscapes. The old city of Pavia to the south of Milan is a significant agricultural centre and is encircled by crops (mainly rice) as much as industrial developments.

Contents

Footnotes

Language

In hotels and bigger restaurants, you'll usually find English is spoken. The further you go from the tourist centres, however, the more trouble you may have, unless you have at least a smattering of Italian. Around the northern shores German is spoken nearly as often as English as a second language.

You'll find that the heavy Veronese dialect is spoken in the east of the region. A slight variant on the Veneto dialect, the dialect spoken today in and around Verona has changed little in centuries and exhibits Germanic influences. Characteristic sounds are short, clipped and nasal, from the back of the mouth. Lombard dialects are scarcely spoken and the few people who keep the language alive will, in most instances, use standard Italian when speaking to someone unfamiliar.

Stress in spoken Italian usually falls on the penultimate syllable. Italian has standard sounds: unlike English you can work out how it sounds from how it's written and vice versa.

Vowels

a	like 'a' in cat	i	like 'i' in sip (except after c or g, see below)
e	like 'e' in vet, or slightly more open, like the 'ai' in air (except after c or g, see consonants below)	o	like 'o' in fox
		u	like 'ou' in soup

Consonants

Generally consonants sound the same as in English, though 'e' and 'i' after 'c' or 'g' make them soft (a 'ch' or a 'j' sound) and are silent themselves, whereas 'h' makes them hard (a 'k' or 'g' sound), the opposite to English. So ciao is pronounced 'chaow', but chiesa (church) is pronounced 'kee-ay-sa'.

The combination 'gli' is pronounced like the 'lli' in million, and 'gn' like 'ny' in Tanya.

Basics

thank you	*grazie*	goodnight	*buonanotte*
hi/goodbye	*ciao* (informal)	goodbye	*arrivederci*
good day		please	*per favore*
(until after lunch/		I'm sorry	*mi dispiace*
mid-afternoon)	*buongiorno*	excuse me	*permesso*
good evening		yes	*si*
(after lunch)	*buonasera*	no	*no*

Numbers

1	uno	17	diciassette
2	due	18	diciotto
3	tre	19	diciannove
4	quattro	20	venti
5	cinque	21	ventuno
6	sei	22	ventidue
7	sette	30	trenta
8	otto	40	quaranta
9	nove	50	cinquanta
10	dieci	60	sessanta
11	undici	70	settanta
12	dodici	80	ottanta
13	tredici	90	novanta
14	quattordici	100	cento
15	quindici	200	due cento
16	sedici	1000	mille

Gestures

Italians are famously theatrical and animated in dialogue and use a variety of gestures.

Side of left palm on side of right wrist as right wrist is flicked up Go away

Hunched shoulders and arms lifted with palms of hands outwards What am I supposed to do?

Thumb, index and middle finger of hand together, wrist upturned and shaking What are you doing/what's going on?

Both palms together and moved up and down in front of stomach Same as above

All fingers of hand squeezed together To signify a place is packed full of people

Front or side of hand to chin 'Nothing', as in 'I don't understand' or 'I've had enough'

Flicking back of right ear To signify someone is gay

Index finger in cheek To signify good food

Questions

how?	come?	where?	dove?
how much?	quanto?	why?	perché?
when?	quando?	what?	che cosa?

Problems

I don't understand	non capisco
I don't know	non lo so
I don't speak Italian	non parlo italiano
How do you say ... (in Italian)?	come si dice ... (in italiano)?
Is there anyone who speaks English?	c'è qualcuno che parla inglese?

Shopping

this one/that one	questo/quello
less	meno
more	di più
how much is it/are they?	quanto costa/costano?
can I have ...?	posso avere ...?

Travelling

one ticket for...	*un biglietto per...*
single	*solo andata*
return	*andata e ritorno*
does this go to Como?	*questo va a Como?*
airport	*aeroporto*
bus stop	*fermata*
train	*treno*
car	*macchina*
taxi	*tassi*

Hotels

a double/single room	*una camera doppia/singola*
a double bed	*un letto matrimoniale*
bathroom	*bagno*
Is there a view?	*c'è un bel panorama?*
can I see the room?	*posso vedere la camera?*
when is breakfast?	*a che ora è la colazione?*
can I have the key?	*posso avere la chiave?*

Restaurants

can I have the bill please?	*posso avere il conto per favore?*
is there a menu?	*c'è un menù?*
what do you recommend?	*che cosa mi consegna?*
what's this?	*cos'è questo?*
where's the toilet?	*dov'è il bagno?*

Time

morning	*mattina*
afternoon	*pomeriggio*
evening	*sera*
night	*notte*
soon	*presto/fra poco*
later	*più tardi*
what time is it?	*che ore sono?*
today/tomorrow/yesterday	*oggi/domani/ieri*

Days

Monday	*lunedi*
Tuesday	*martedi*
Wednesday	*mercoledi*
Thursday	*giovedi*
Friday	*venerdi*
Saturday	*sabato*
Sunday	*domenica*

Conversation

alright	*va bene*
right then	*allora*
who knows!	*bo!/chi sa*
good luck!	*in bocca al lupo!*
	(literally, 'in the mouth of the wolf')
one moment	*un attimo*
hello (when answering a phone)	*pronto* (literally, 'ready')
let's go!	*andiamo!*
enough/stop	*basta!*
give up!	*dai!*
I like ...	*mi piace ...*
how's it going?	*come va?*
(well, thanks)	*(bene, grazie)*
how are you?	*come sta/stai?* (polite/informal)

Menu reader

General

affumicato smoked
al sangue rare
alla griglia grilled
antipasto starter/appetizer
aperto/chiuso open/closed
arrosto roasted
ben cotto well done
bollito boiled
caldo hot
cameriere/cameriera waiter/waitress
conto the bill
contorni side dishes
coperto cover charge
coppa/cono cone/cup
cotto cooked
cottura media medium
crudo raw
degustazione tasting menu of several dishes
dolce dessert
fatto in casa home-made
forno a legna wood-fired oven
freddo cold
fresco fresh, uncooked
fritto fried
menu turistico tourist menu
piccante spicy
prenotazione reservation
primo first course
ripieno a stuffing or something that is stuffed
secondo second course

Drinks (*bevande*)

acqua naturale/gassata/frizzante
still/sparkling water
aperitivo drinks taken before dinner,
often served with free snacks
bicchiere glass
birra beer
birra alla spina draught beer
bottiglia bottle
caffè coffee (ie espresso)
caffè macchiato/ristretto espresso with a
dash of foamed milk/strong
spremuta freshly squeezed fruit juice

succo juice
vino bianco/rosato/rosso white/rosé/red wine

Fruit (*frutta*) and vegetables (*legumi*)

agrumi citrus fruits
amarena sour cherry
arancia orange
carciofio globe artichoke
castagne chestnuts
cipolle onions
cocomero water melon
contorno side dish, usually grilled
vegetables or oven-baked potatoes
fichi figs
finocchio fennel
fragole strawberries
friarelli strong flavoured leaves of the
broccoli family eaten with sausages
frutta fresca fresh fruit
funghi mushroom
lamponi raspberries
melagrana pomegranate
melanzana eggplant/aubergine
melone light coloured melon
mele apples
noci/nocciole walnuts/hazelnuts
patate potatoes, which can be *arroste* (roast),
fritte (fried), *novelle* (new), *pure' di* (mashed)
patatine fritte chips
peperoncino chilli pepper
peperone peppers
pesche peaches
piselli peas
pomodoro tomato
rucola rocket
scarola leafy green vegetable used in *torta
di scarola* pie
sciurilli or *fiorilli* tempura courgette flowers
spinaci spinach
verdure vegetables
zucca pumpkin

Meat (*carne*)

affettati misti mixed cured meat
agnello lamb
bistecca beef steak

bresaola thinly sliced, air-cured beef from Valtellina

carpaccio finely sliced raw meat (usually beef)

cinghiale boar

coda alla vaccinara oxtail

coniglio rabbit

involtini thinly sliced meat, rolled and stuffed

manzo beef

pollo chicken

polpette meatballs

polpettone meat loaf

porchetta roasted whole suckling pig

prosciutto ham – *cotto* cooked, *crudo* cured

salsicce pork sausage

salumi cured meats, usually served mixed (*salumi misto*) on a wooden platter

speck a type of cured, smoked ham

spiedini meat pieces grilled on a skewer

stufato meat stew

trippa tripe

vitello veal

Fish (*pesce*) and seafood (*frutti di mare*)

acciughe anchovies

aragosta lobster

baccalà salt cod

bottarga mullet-roe

branzino sea bass

calamari squid

cozze mussels

frittura di mare/frittura di paranza small fish, squid and shellfish lightly covered with flour and fried

frutti di mare seafood

gamberi shrimps/prawns

grigliata mista di pesce mixed grilled fish

orata gilt-head/sea bream

ostriche oysters

pesce spada swordfish

polpo octopus

sarde, sardine sardines

seppia cuttlefish

sogliola sole

spigola bass

stoccafisso stockfish

tonno tuna

triglia red mullet

trota trout

vongole clams

Dessert (*dolce*)

cornetto sweet croissant

crema custard

dolce dessert

gelato ice cream

granita flavoured crushed ice

macedonia (di frutta) fruit cocktail dessert with white wine

panettone type of fruit bread eaten at Christmas

semifreddo a partially frozen dessert

sorbetto sorbet

tiramisù rich 'pick-me-up' dessert

torta cake

zabaglione whipped egg yolks flavoured with Marsala wine

zuppa inglese English-style trifle

Other

aceto balsamico balsamic vinegar, usually from Modena

arborio type of rice used to make risotto

burro butter

calzone pizza dough rolled with the chef's choice of filling and then baked

casatiello lard bread

fagioli white beans

formaggi misti mixed cheese plate

formaggio cheese

frittata omelette

insalata salad

insalata Caprese salad of tomatoes, mozzarella and basil

latte milk

lenticchie lentils

mandorla almond

miele honey

olio oil

polenta cornmeal

pane bread

pane-integrale brown bread

pinoli pine nuts

provola cheese, sometimes with a smoky flavour

ragù a meaty sauce or ragout

riso rice

salsa sauce

sugo sauce or gravy

zuppa soup

Architectural glossary

aedicule frame around a doorway or window comprised of columns or pilasters and an entablature on top, typical of Classical and Gothic architecture; could be a mini decorative structure housing a statue.

arcade row of columns that support arches.

architrave lower part of an entablature, which meets the capitals of the columns.

baldachin canopy over a tomb, supported by columns.

campanile bell tower.

capital top or 'crown' of a column, often adorned with scrolls (Ionic) or acanthus leaves (Corinthian).

cloister open covered passage around a courtyard (usually part of a church or monastery), supported by columns or arches.

columns the Greek order of columns include Doric, plain with vertical grooves called fluting; Ionic, characterized by scrolls; and Corinthian, with a bell-shaped capital, often adorned with acanthus leaves and volutes. The Roman's Tuscan order are without decoration, while the Composite order was a mishmash of the three Grecian orders.

choir chancel of a church, used by the clergy and choir, occasionally separated from the nave by a screen.

colonnade series of columns.

cornice horizontal ledge or moulding. For practical purposes it's a gutter, draining water off the building, or a decorative feature if purely aesthetic.

cupola dome on a roof.

entablature held up by columns, the entablature includes the architrave, frieze and cornice.

frieze centre of an entablature; often decorated.

loggia open ground floor gallery, recessed gallery, or corridor on the façade of a building.

nave central body of the church, between the aisles.

narthex long porch along the entrance of a church, before the nave.

pilaster rectangular column that only slightly protrudes from a wall.

pinnacle small, often ornate, turret, popular in Gothic architecture.

plinth lower part or base of a column.

portico doorway, often roofed, serving as an entrance (real or decorative) to a building.

sacristy room off the main or side altars in a church or a separate building housing sacred vessels, vestments and records.

tracery ornamental stonework that supports the glass in Gothic windows.

Notes

Index

Titles available in the Footprint *Focus* range

Latin America	UK RRP	US RRP
Bahia & Salvador	£7.99	$11.95
Brazilian Amazon	£7.99	$11.95
Brazilian Pantanal	£6.99	$9.95
Buenos Aires & Pampas	£7.99	$11.95
Cartagena & Caribbean Coast	£7.99	$11.95
Costa Rica	£8.99	$12.95
Cuzco, La Paz & Lake Titicaca	£8.99	$12.95
El Salvador	£5.99	$8.95
Guadalajara & Pacific Coast	£6.99	$9.95
Guatemala	£8.99	$12.95
Guyana, Guyane & Suriname	£5.99	$8.95
Havana	£6.99	$9.95
Honduras	£7.99	$11.95
Nicaragua	£7.99	$11.95
Northeast Argentina & Uruguay	£8.99	$12.95
Paraguay	£5.99	$8.95
Quito & Galápagos Islands	£7.99	$11.95
Recife & Northeast Brazil	£7.99	$11.95
Rio de Janeiro	£8.99	$12.95
São Paulo	£5.99	$8.95
Uruguay	£6.99	$9.95
Venezuela	£8.99	$12.95
Yucatán Peninsula	£6.99	$9.95

Asia	UK RRP	US RRP
Angkor Wat	£5.99	$8.95
Bali & Lombok	£8.99	$12.95
Chennai & Tamil Nadu	£8.99	$12.95
Chiang Mai & Northern Thailand	£7.99	$11.95
Goa	£6.99	$9.95
Gulf of Thailand	£8.99	$12.95
Hanoi & Northern Vietnam	£8.99	$12.95
Ho Chi Minh City & Mekong Delta	£7.99	$11.95
Java	£7.99	$11.95
Kerala	£7.99	$11.95
Kolkata & West Bengal	£5.99	$8.95
Mumbai & Gujarat	£8.99	$12.95

Africa & Middle East	UK RRP	US RRP
Beirut	£6.99	$9.95
Cairo & Nile Delta	£8.99	$12.95
Damascus	£5.99	$8.95
Durban & KwaZulu Natal	£8.99	$12.95
Fès & Northern Morocco	£8.99	$12.95
Jerusalem	£8.99	$12.95
Johannesburg & Kruger National Park	£7.99	$11.95
Kenya's Beaches	£8.99	$12.95
Kilimanjaro & Northern Tanzania	£8.99	$12.95
Luxor to Aswan	£8.99	$12.95
Nairobi & Rift Valley	£7.99	$11.95
Red Sea & Sinai	£7.99	$11.95
Zanzibar & Pemba	£7.99	$11.95

Europe	UK RRP	US RRP
Bilbao & Basque Region	£6.99	$9.95
Brittany West Coast	£7.99	$11.95
Cádiz & Costa de la Luz	£6.99	$9.95
Granada & Sierra Nevada	£6.99	$9.95
Languedoc: Carcassonne to Montpellier	£7.99	$11.95
Málaga	£5.99	$8.95
Marseille & Western Provence	£7.99	$11.95
Orkney & Shetland Islands	£5.99	$8.95
Santander & Picos de Europa	£7.99	$11.95
Sardinia: Alghero & the North	£7.99	$11.95
Sardinia: Cagliari & the South	£7.99	$11.95
Seville	£5.99	$8.95
Sicily: Palermo & the Northwest	£7.99	$11.95
Sicily: Catania & the Southeast	£7.99	$11.95
Siena & Southern Tuscany	£7.99	$11.95
Sorrento, Capri & Amalfi Coast	£6.99	$9.95
Skye & Outer Hebrides	£6.99	$9.95
Verona & Lake Garda	£7.99	$11.95

North America	UK RRP	US RRP
Vancouver & Rockies	£8.99	$12.95

Australasia	UK RRP	US RRP
Brisbane & Queensland	£8.99	$12.95
Perth	£7.99	$11.95

For the latest books, e-books and a wealth of travel information, visit us at: www.footprinttravelguides.com.

footprinttravelguides.com

Join us on facebook for the latest travel news, product releases, offers and amazing competitions: www.facebook.com/footprintbooks.